# IOT FOR BEGINNERS: A STEP BY STEP GUIDE

S.KOKILA

D.ANNIE SELINA

A.SUMATHI

Made with ♥ on the Notion Press Platform
www.notionpress.com

# Contents

# ONE

# INTRODUCTION

Imagine a world where your refrigerator automatically orders groceries when you're running low, your home adjusts its temperature based on your location, and your city optimizes traffic flow based on real-time data. This isn't science fiction; it's the reality of the Internet of Things (IoT), a transformative technology that's rapidly reshaping our lives. We're living in an era where everyday objects, from light bulbs to industrial machinery, are becoming intelligent and interconnected, creating a vast network of information and automation. But where do you begin in this ever-expanding universe of connected things? That's precisely what this book is for. "IoT for Beginners: A Step-by-Step Guide" is your comprehensive introduction to the fascinating world of IoT, designed to demystify its complexities and empower you to build your own connected projects. Whether you're a student, a hobbyist, or a professional eager to explore the potential of IoT, this book will provide you with the essential knowledge and practical skills to embark on your journey.

The impact of IoT is undeniable. From smart homes and wearable devices to industrial automation and smart cities, IoT is revolutionizing industries and transforming the way we interact with our environment. But beyond the buzzwords and hype, what exactly is IoT, and why does it matter? At its core, IoT is about connecting physical devices to the internet, enabling them to collect, exchange, and act upon data. This connectivity unlocks a wealth of possibilities, from optimizing energy consumption and improving healthcare to enhancing productivity and creating entirely new business models. In this book, we'll delve into the fundamental concepts of IoT, exploring its architecture, communication protocols, and security considerations. You'll learn how to choose the right development platforms, work with sensors and actuators, and build practical IoT projects from scratch. We'll guide you through the process of setting up your development environment, writing code, and connecting your devices to the cloud. You'll learn to understand how to store, display, and process data.

This isn't just a theoretical exploration; it's a hands-on learning experience. We believe that the best way to understand IoT is by building real-world projects. That's why this book is packed with practical examples and step-by-step tutorials that will guide you through the process of creating your own IoT solutions. You'll start with simple projects, such as a smart home temperature monitoring system and a remote-controlled LED, and gradually progress to more complex applications, like a motion-activated security system. We'll also cover cloud platforms, and mobile integration. We'll cover the basic building blocks and get you to a point where you can explore on your own. Each chapter is designed to build upon the previous one, providing a clear and logical progression through the world of IoT. We'll break down complex concepts into manageable chunks, providing clear explanations and practical examples along the way. We'll also give you troubleshooting tips, which will help you navigate the common roadblocks that beginners often encounter.

The world of IoT is constantly evolving, with new technologies and applications emerging every day. By mastering the fundamentals of IoT, you'll be well-equipped to embrace the future of connectivity and contribute to this exciting field. This book is your starting point, your guide, and your companion on this journey. We encourage you to experiment, explore, and let your creativity guide you. Whether your goal is to build a smart home, develop innovative IoT solutions for your business, or simply satisfy your curiosity, this book will provide you with the knowledge and skills you need to succeed. So, let's embark on this exciting adventure together and unlock the limitless potential of the Internet of Things. Let's begin building the future, one connected device at a time.

# TWO
# UNDERSTANDING THE INTERNET OF THINGS (IOT)

A world increasingly defined by connection. Not just between people, but between things. The Internet of Things (IoT) is the invisible web that weaves together our physical world with the digital realm, transforming everyday objects into intelligent, data-driven entities. While the term itself might seem futuristic, the impact of IoT is already deeply woven into our daily lives, from the smartwatches on our wrists to the traffic lights that optimize our commutes. But what lies beneath the surface of this interconnected landscape? What are the fundamental principles that drive IoT, and how does it reshape our understanding of technology and its potential? This book, "Understanding the Internet of Things (IoT)," is dedicated to answering these questions, providing a comprehensive exploration of the core concepts that define this revolutionary field. We will move beyond the superficial and delve into the very essence of what makes IoT tick, revealing the intricate mechanisms that enable seamless communication and data exchange between devices.

To truly understand IoT, we must first dissect its fundamental components. This isn't just about connecting devices; it's about creating a cohesive ecosystem where data flows freely, enabling real-time insights and automated actions. We'll begin by exploring the core architecture of IoT, from the sensors and actuators that gather data to the cloud platforms that process and analyze it. We'll unravel the complexities of communication protocols, examining the diverse range of technologies that enable devices to communicate with each other and the cloud. We'll also address the crucial topic of security, understanding the inherent risks and the essential measures required to protect our interconnected world. We will also explore the different types of data that are being collected, and how that data is used. By understanding these core principles, you'll gain a deeper appreciation for the intricate dance of data that powers the IoT revolution. We will also explore the evolution of IoT, and how it has changed over the past few decades.

The true power of IoT lies in its diverse and ever-expanding applications. From smart homes that anticipate our needs to industrial systems that optimize production, IoT is transforming industries and reshaping our daily lives. We'll explore the practical applications of IoT across various sectors, demonstrating how this technology is being used to solve real-world problems and create new opportunities. We'll examine the impact of IoT on healthcare, transportation, agriculture, and manufacturing, showcasing the innovative solutions that are emerging in each field. We'll also consider the ethical implications of IoT, exploring the challenges and opportunities that arise from the increasing collection and analysis of data. We'll delve into the societal impact of IoT, considering the ways in which this technology is changing the way we live, work, and interact with the world around us. We will explore the idea of edge computing, and how it is changing the way IoT data is processed.

Understanding the Internet of Things is not just about grasping the current state of technology; it's about building a foundation for future innovation. As IoT continues to evolve, new possibilities will emerge, driven by advancements in artificial intelligence, machine learning, and other cutting-edge technologies. By equipping yourself with a solid understanding of the core principles of IoT, you'll be well-prepared to navigate this rapidly changing landscape and contribute to the development of innovative solutions. This book is your guide to understanding the fundamental building blocks of IoT, providing you with the knowledge and insights you need to explore the limitless potential of this transformative technology. Let's embark on a journey to demystify the complexities of IoT and unlock the power of connected things. By the end of this journey, you will have a solid understanding of how IOT works, and its potential impact on the future.

# THREE

## CONNECTING THE PHYSICAL WORLD

Imagine a world where the boundaries between the digital and physical realms dissolve, where everyday objects possess an intelligence that allows them to perceive, communicate, and react to their surroundings. This isn't a futuristic fantasy; it's the burgeoning reality of "Connecting the Physical World," a concept at the heart of the Internet of Things (IoT). We've long been accustomed to the internet as a space for information and communication between people, but the true revolution lies in extending this connectivity to the tangible world we inhabit. From the gentle hum of a smart thermostat anticipating our comfort to the intricate network of sensors monitoring the structural integrity of a bridge, we are witnessing the emergence of a world where physical objects are becoming active participants in the digital ecosystem. This paradigm shift, the act of connecting the physical world, is not merely about adding internet access to devices; it's about fundamentally altering our relationship with the objects around us, infusing them with a digital awareness that unlocks a new era of efficiency, insight, and automation. This concept, fundamentally, is about taking the data of the real world, and making it actionable.

The act of connecting the physical world transcends the mere collection of data; it's about transforming that data into meaningful action. It's about empowering our environment to respond to our needs, anticipate potential problems, and optimize processes in ways previously unimaginable. Consider the implications for industries, where connected sensors can monitor machinery for signs of wear and tear, predicting failures before they occur and minimizing downtime. Or envision the impact on agriculture, where smart irrigation systems can optimize water usage based on real-time soil moisture data, leading to increased yields and reduced waste. The beauty of connecting the physical world lies not just in the sheer volume of data it generates, but in the actionable insights it provides. This connectivity is the foundation upon which we build smart cities, responsive healthcare systems, and sustainable energy solutions. It is the bridge that allows us to move beyond passive observation of our environment to active participation in shaping it. We are not simply connecting devices; we are connecting potential, we are connecting solutions, and we are connecting the future. By embracing the power of physical connectivity, we embark on a journey towards a more efficient, intelligent, and interconnected world, where the boundaries between the digital and physical realms become increasingly blurred, and the possibilities become truly limitless.

## THE ESSENCE OF INTERCONNECTION

The Internet of Things (IoT) is more than just a buzzword; it's a fundamental shift in how we interact with technology and the world around us. At its core, IoT is about extending internet connectivity beyond traditional devices like computers and smartphones to a vast array of physical objects. This interconnection allows these objects to collect and exchange data, enabling them to sense, communicate, and react to their environment. Defining IoT requires understanding that it's not just about connecting "things," but about creating a network of intelligent devices that work together to provide valuable insights and automated actions. It's the bridge between the digital and physical worlds. The goal of this connection is to make the physical world more efficient, responsive, and intelligent.

To truly define IoT, we must consider several key principles:

- **Connectivity:** IoT devices are connected to the internet or other networks, enabling them to transmit and receive data. This connectivity can be achieved through various technologies, including Wi-Fi, Bluetooth, cellular networks, and low-power wide-area networks (LPWANs).
- **Sensing:** IoT devices often incorporate sensors that collect data about their surroundings. These sensors can measure a wide range of parameters, such as temperature, humidity, light, motion, and pressure.
- **Data Processing:** The data collected by IoT devices is processed and analyzed, either locally or in the cloud. This processing can involve simple tasks, such as filtering and formatting data, or more complex tasks, such as machine learning and artificial intelligence.
- **Action and Automation:** Based on the processed data, IoT devices can take actions, such as controlling actuators, sending alerts, or triggering automated processes. This automation can improve efficiency, safety, and convenience.
- **Uniqueness:** Each IoT device is uniquely identifiable through its IP address or other identifiers, allowing it to be addressed and managed within the network.

The definition of IoT goes beyond simply connecting devices. It encompasses the concept of intelligence and autonomy. IoT devices are not just passive data collectors; they are capable of making decisions and taking actions based on the information they gather. This intelligence can be embedded within the devices themselves (edge computing) or reside in the cloud. The ability of IoT devices to learn and adapt is a crucial aspect of their definition. Machine learning and artificial intelligence are increasingly being integrated into IoT systems, enabling them to analyze vast amounts of data and identify patterns that would be difficult for humans to detect. This leads to predictive maintenance, optimized energy consumption, and other advanced applications.

The scope of IoT is constantly expanding, encompassing a wide range of devices and applications. From smart home appliances to industrial machinery, IoT is transforming industries and reshaping our daily lives. The definition of IoT is not static; it is evolving as new technologies and applications emerge. As we continue to connect more and more devices, the boundaries of IoT will continue to expand, creating a truly interconnected world. The future of IoT is about creating a seamless and intelligent environment where devices work together to enhance our lives.

## KEY COMPONENTS OF AN IOT SYSTEM

### The Architectural Foundation

An IoT system is a complex ecosystem that comprises several key components working together to enable data collection, processing, and action. Understanding these components is essential for building and deploying effective IoT solutions. The architecture of an IoT system can be broadly divided into four main layers: devices and sensors, connectivity and gateways, cloud platforms, and applications and user interfaces. Each layer plays a crucial role in the overall functionality of the system.

### Devices and Sensors

- **Sensors:** These are the primary data collectors in an IoT system. They measure various physical parameters, such as temperature, humidity, light, motion, and pressure. Sensors can be analog or digital, and they can be integrated into a wide range of devices.
- **Actuators:** These are devices that take actions based on the data received. They can control physical processes, such as turning on lights, adjusting thermostats, or activating motors.
- **Embedded Systems:** These are the microcontrollers and microprocessors that control the operation of IoT devices. They are responsible for collecting data from sensors, processing it, and sending it to the cloud. They also receive commands from

the cloud and control actuators.

## Connectivity and Gateways

- **Connectivity:** This layer enables communication between IoT devices and the cloud. Various connectivity technologies are used, including Wi-Fi, Bluetooth, cellular networks, and LPWANs. The choice of connectivity technology depends on the specific requirements of the application.
- **Gateways:** These are devices that act as intermediaries between IoT devices and the cloud. They aggregate data from multiple devices, perform local processing, and forward data to the cloud. Gateways can also provide security and management functions.

## Cloud Platforms and Applications

- **Cloud Platforms:** These provide the infrastructure for storing, processing, and analyzing IoT data. They offer services such as data storage, data analytics, device management, and application development. Examples include AWS IoT Core, Azure IoT Hub, and Google Cloud IoT Core.
- **Applications and User Interfaces:** These are the software applications that allow users to interact with the IoT system. They provide visualizations of data, control devices, and manage the overall system. User interfaces can be web-based, mobile apps, or other types of applications. The data that is collected in the cloud can then be used to train machine learning models, and create advanced analytics. The value of an IOT system is directly related to how well all of these parts communicate.

### THE EVOLUTION OF IOT

The concept of connected devices has been around for decades, but the term "Internet of Things" was coined by Kevin Ashton in 1999. The evolution of IoT can be traced back to the early days of the internet, when researchers began exploring the possibility of connecting physical objects to the network. Early examples include automated teller machines (ATMs) and industrial control systems. However, the widespread adoption of IoT was limited by the high cost of hardware and the lack of standardized communication protocols.

### The Rise of Enabling Technologies

Several key technologies have driven the evolution of IoT:

- **Microcontrollers and Sensors**: The development of low-cost, low-power microcontrollers and sensors has made it possible to embed intelligence into a wide range of devices.
- **Wireless Communication**: The proliferation of wireless communication technologies, such as Wi-Fi, Bluetooth, and cellular networks, has enabled devices to connect to the internet without the need for physical cables.
- **Cloud Computing**: Cloud platforms have provided the infrastructure for storing, processing, and analyzing the vast amounts of data generated by IoT devices.
- **Big Data and Analytics:** Advances in big data and analytics have made it possible to extract valuable insights from IoT data.

### Key Milestones and Developments

The evolution of IoT has been marked by several key milestones:

- The early 2000s saw the emergence of RFID (Radio-Frequency Identification) technology, which enabled the tracking of objects using radio waves.
- The mid-2000s saw the development of wireless sensor networks (WSNs), which enabled the deployment of large numbers of sensors in remote locations.
- The late 2000s saw the rise of cloud computing, which provided the infrastructure for storing and processing IoT data.
- The 2010s saw the rapid growth of the consumer IoT market, with the introduction of smart home devices, wearable devices, and connected cars.

- The late 2010's and early 2020's saw the rise of industrial IOT, and the increase of security concerns.

**The Future of IoT**

The future of IoT is about creating a truly connected world where devices work together to enhance our lives. As technologies continue to advance, we can expect to see even more innovative IoT applications emerge. The evolution of IoT is ongoing, and it will continue to shape the way we live and work. The integration of artificial intelligence, machine learning, and edge computing will further enhance the capabilities of IoT systems. The future of IoT is about creating a seamless and intelligent environment where devices work together to enhance our lives.

**REAL-WORLD APPLICATIONS OF IOT: FROM HOMES TO INDUSTRIES**

**1. Transforming Daily Life: Smart Homes and Beyond**

The impact of the Internet of Things (IoT) is immediately apparent in our daily lives, particularly within the realm of smart homes. These interconnected environments are designed to enhance comfort, convenience, and efficiency through automated and remotely controlled devices. Imagine waking up to a coffee maker that starts brewing automatically based on your alarm, or a thermostat that adjusts the temperature according to your preferences and schedule. Smart lighting systems can optimize energy consumption by dimming or turning off lights when rooms are unoccupied, while security cameras and door locks provide enhanced safety and peace of mind. Beyond the home, wearable devices like smartwatches and fitness trackers are revolutionizing personal health monitoring. These devices track vital signs, activity levels, and sleep patterns, providing users with valuable insights into their well-being. Connected cars are another significant application, offering features such as real-time traffic updates, navigation assistance, and remote diagnostics. These applications demonstrate the transformative power of IoT in making our daily lives more convenient, efficient, and personalized. The data gathered from these devices is used to make decisions that improve the lives of the user.

### 2. Revolutionizing Industries

The Industrial Internet of Things (IIoT) is transforming industries by connecting machines, sensors, and data analytics to optimize operations and improve efficiency. In manufacturing, IIoT enables predictive maintenance, where sensors monitor machinery for signs of wear and tear, predicting failures before they occur. This minimizes downtime, reduces maintenance costs, and improves overall productivity. Smart factories are leveraging IIoT to automate production processes, optimize resource utilization, and improve product quality. In the energy sector, smart grids are using IoT to monitor and manage power distribution, enabling more efficient and reliable energy delivery. Sensors deployed in pipelines and power plants can detect leaks and malfunctions, preventing costly and potentially hazardous incidents. In agriculture, precision farming is using IoT to optimize crop yields and resource management. Sensors monitor soil moisture, temperature, and nutrient levels, enabling farmers to make data-driven decisions about irrigation, fertilization, and pest control. Logistics and supply chain management are also benefiting from IIoT, with real-time tracking of goods, optimized routing, and improved inventory management. The IIoT is about using data to make better decisions in an industrial setting.

### 3. Smart Cities: Building Sustainable and Efficient Urban Environments

Smart cities are leveraging IoT to create sustainable and efficient urban environments. Connected sensors and devices are used to monitor and manage various aspects of city infrastructure, including traffic flow, waste management, and energy consumption. Smart traffic management systems use sensors and cameras to monitor traffic patterns, adjusting traffic lights and providing real-time information to drivers to reduce congestion. Smart waste management systems use sensors to monitor fill levels in trash bins, optimizing collection routes and reducing waste.

Smart lighting systems adjust streetlights based on ambient light and pedestrian activity, reducing energy consumption and improving safety. Environmental monitoring systems use sensors to track air and water quality, providing data to inform policy decisions and protect public health. Public safety is also enhanced through IoT applications, such as surveillance cameras, gunshot detection systems, and emergency response systems. The data from these systems is used to improve the quality of life for the people living in the city. Smart parking systems use sensors to monitor parking availability, guiding drivers to available spaces and reducing search times. Smart cities are about using data to make cities more livable.

### 4. Healthcare and Beyond: Expanding the Boundaries of IoT

The healthcare sector is witnessing a significant transformation through the application of IoT. Remote patient monitoring devices enable healthcare providers to track patients' vital signs and health conditions remotely, improving patient outcomes and reducing hospital readmissions. Connected medical devices, such as insulin pumps and pacemakers, provide real-time data and enable remote adjustments, improving patient care and quality of life. In retail, IoT is used to enhance the customer experience and optimize operations. Smart shelves use sensors to track inventory levels, providing real-time data to retailers and preventing stockouts. In transportation, IoT is used to improve safety and efficiency. Connected vehicles communicate with each other and with infrastructure, enabling features such as collision avoidance and adaptive cruise control. In environmental monitoring, IoT is used to track pollution levels, monitor wildlife populations, and predict natural disasters. Sensors deployed in remote locations provide data to inform conservation efforts and disaster preparedness. The applications of IoT are vast and continue to expand as new technologies and innovations emerge. The use of IoT is only limited by the imagination. As more devices become connected, the possibilities for innovation and improvement will continue to grow.

# FOUR

# THE ARCHITECTURE OF IOT

The Internet of Things (IoT), with its promise of seamless connectivity and intelligent automation, relies on a carefully designed architectural framework. This architecture is not a monolithic entity but rather a layered structure, a blueprint that dictates how devices communicate, data is processed, and insights are delivered. Understanding this architecture is crucial for anyone seeking to build, deploy, or simply comprehend the inner workings of an IoT system. It's the foundation upon which the entire ecosystem of connected devices rests, a framework that ensures data flows smoothly, decisions are made efficiently, and users experience the benefits of interconnected intelligence. We're not merely connecting devices; we're constructing a complex and dynamic network, a symphony of hardware and software that harmonizes to create a cohesive and functional whole. This section of the book is designed to illuminate this framework, to peel back the layers and reveal the essential components that make IoT a reality. It is the core set of rules that allow the physical world to communicate with the digital world.

The architecture of IoT can be visualized as a series of interconnected layers, each playing a vital role in the overall system. From the humble sensors collecting data at the edge to the powerful cloud platforms processing and analyzing that information, each layer contributes to the seamless flow of data and the delivery of actionable insights. We'll explore the role of devices and sensors, the data collectors that form the foundation of IoT systems. We'll delve into the intricacies of connectivity and gateways, the bridges that connect these devices to the cloud. We'll examine the capabilities of cloud platforms, the data processors and storage facilities that transform raw data into valuable information. And finally, we'll explore the applications and user interfaces, the gateways through which humans interact with the IoT ecosystem. This journey through the architectural layers will provide you with a comprehensive understanding of how these components work together to create a cohesive and functional IoT system. We will explore how information is passed between these layers, and how each layer plays a vital role in the overall function of the system. This is the understanding of the design that enables the creation of successful IoT products.

**DEVICES AND SENSORS**

Devices and sensors form the bedrock of any IoT system. They are the physical interfaces that interact with the real world, collecting the raw data that fuels the entire ecosystem. These components are responsible for transforming physical phenomena into digital signals that can be processed and analyzed. A "device" in IoT can range from a simple temperature sensor to a complex industrial machine, while "sensors" are the specific elements within these devices that detect and measure physical properties. The primary function of these data collectors is to perceive and quantify changes in their environment, providing the necessary input for informed decision-making.

**Sensor Types and Processes**

**Temperature Sensors:**

- Process: Measure the degree of hotness or coldness. Types include thermocouples, thermistors, and resistance temperature detectors (RTDs).
- Benefits: Enables climate control, process monitoring, and safety applications.

**Humidity Sensors:**

- Process: Measure the moisture content in the air. Types include capacitive, resistive, and thermal conductivity sensors.
- Benefits: Crucial for agriculture, HVAC systems, and weather forecasting.

**Motion Sensors:**

- Process: Detect movement or changes in position. Types include passive infrared (PIR), ultrasonic, and accelerometer sensors.
- Benefits: Used in security systems, automated lighting, and activity tracking.

**Light Sensors:**

- Process: Measure the intensity of light. Types include photoresistors, photodiodes, and phototransistors.
- Benefits: Used in automatic lighting, camera systems, and environmental monitoring.

**Pressure Sensors:**

- Process: Measure the force applied over an area. Types include piezoresistive, capacitive, and strain gauge sensors.
- Benefits: Used in industrial automation, medical devices, and automotive applications.

## Gas Sensors:

- Process: Detect the presence and concentration of specific gases. Types include electrochemical, semiconductor, and optical sensors.
- Benefits: Used in air quality monitoring, industrial safety, and leak detection.

## Device Types and Processes
## Wearable Devices:

- Process: Collect health and activity data. Examples include smartwatches, fitness trackers, and medical sensors.
- Benefits: Personal health monitoring, activity tracking, and remote patient care.

## Smart Home Appliances:

- Process: Automate home functions, such as lighting, heating, and security. Examples include smart thermostats, lights, and cameras.
- Benefits: Increased comfort, convenience, and energy efficiency.

## Industrial Machines:

- Process: Monitor and control industrial processes, such as manufacturing, energy production, and logistics. Examples include robotic arms, conveyor systems, and monitoring equipment.
- Benefits: Improved efficiency, productivity, and safety.

## Environmental Monitoring Devices:

- ○ Process: Monitor environmental conditions, such as air and water quality. Examples include weather stations, pollution sensors, and water quality monitors.
- ○ Benefits: Environmental protection, disaster prevention, and public health.

**Automotive Devices:**

- ○ Process: Collect data for vehicle performance, safety, and navigation. Examples include GPS trackers, engine sensors, and collision avoidance systems.
- ○ Benefits: Enhanced safety, efficiency, and driver assistance.

**Benefits of Data Collection**

- Sensors provide up-to-the-minute data, allowing for immediate responses to changing conditions.
- Data analysis can identify patterns that predict equipment failures, reducing downtime and maintenance costs.
- Data-driven insights can improve efficiency and productivity in various industries.
- Sensors can detect hazardous conditions, preventing accidents and protecting lives.
- Wearable devices and smart home appliances can tailor experiences to individual needs and preferences.
- Data can optimize the use of resources, such as energy, water, and materials.

**Challenges and Future Trends**

- **Power Consumption:** Many sensors and devices require low power consumption for long-term operation.
- **Data Accuracy and Reliability:** Ensuring the accuracy and reliability of sensor data is crucial for effective decision-making.

- **Sensor Calibration and Maintenance:** Regular calibration and maintenance are necessary to maintain sensor accuracy.
- **Miniaturization and Integration:** Advancements in microelectronics are enabling the development of smaller and more integrated sensors.
- **Edge Computing:** Processing data closer to the source can reduce latency and bandwidth requirements.
- **AI-Powered Sensors:** Integrating artificial intelligence into sensors can enable more advanced data analysis and decision-making.

## CONNECTIVITY AND GATEWAYS

Connectivity and gateways are the vital bridge between IoT devices and the cloud, enabling the seamless flow of data. Without robust connectivity, the vast amount of data collected by sensors would remain isolated and unusable. Gateways act as intermediaries, aggregating data from multiple devices, performing local processing, and forwarding it to the cloud. This layer ensures that data is transmitted reliably and efficiently, regardless of the distance or complexity of the network.

**Connectivity Technologies and Processes**

**Wi-Fi:**

- Process: Uses radio waves to transmit data over short to medium distances.
- Benefits: High bandwidth, widely available, suitable for indoor environments.
- Types: 802.11 a/b/g/n/ac/ax

**Bluetooth:**

- Process: Uses short-range radio waves for data exchange between devices.
- Benefits: Low power consumption, suitable for personal area networks (PANs).

- Types: Bluetooth Low Energy (BLE), Bluetooth 5.0.

**Cellular Networks (4G/5G/NB-IoT):**

- Process: Uses cellular towers to transmit data over long distances.
- Benefits: Wide coverage, reliable connectivity, suitable for outdoor and remote locations.
- Types: LTE, NB-IoT, 5G.

**Zigbee:**

- Process: Uses low-power radio waves for mesh networking.
- Benefits: Low power consumption, suitable for home automation and industrial applications.

**LoRaWAN:**

- Process: Uses low-power wide-area network (LPWAN) technology for long-range communication.
- Benefits: Long range, low power consumption, suitable for remote monitoring.

**Ethernet:**

- Process: Uses wired connections for high-speed data transmission.
- Benefits: High bandwidth, reliable, suitable for industrial and enterprise applications.

**Gateways and Processes**

- **Data Aggregation:** Gateways collect data from multiple devices and consolidate it into a single stream.

- **Protocol Translation:** Gateways convert data from one protocol to another, enabling communication between devices that use different standards.
- **Edge Computing:** Gateways perform local processing of data, reducing latency and bandwidth requirements.
- **Security:** Gateways provide security features, such as encryption and authentication, to protect data from unauthorized access.
- **Device Management:** Gateways manage the configuration and updates of connected devices.
- **Filtering and pre-processing:** Gateways can filter out unneeded data, and perform initial processing of data before sending it to the cloud.

## Benefits of Connectivity and Gateways

- Enables the reliable and efficient transmission of data between devices and the cloud.
- Edge computing reduces the time it takes to process data, enabling real-time responses.
- Gateways provide security features that protect data from unauthorized access.
- Redundant connectivity options ensure that data is transmitted even in the event of network failures.
- Gateways can manage a large number of connected devices, enabling the deployment of large-scale IoT systems.
- Using gateways to perform local processing can reduce the amount of data transmitted to the cloud, reducing bandwidth costs.

## Challenges and Future Trends

- **Interoperability:** Ensuring that devices from different manufacturers can communicate with each other.

- **Network Congestion:** Managing the increasing amount of data transmitted over networks.
- **Power Consumption:** Optimizing the power consumption of connectivity technologies.
- **5G and LPWANs:** The continued development of 5G and LPWAN technologies will enable more advanced IoT applications.
- **Software Defined Networks (SDN):** SDN enables more flexible and scalable network management.
- **Mesh Networks:** Mesh networks provide redundant connectivity and improved reliability.

## CLOUD PLATFORMS

### The Central Nervous System of IoT

Cloud platforms are the backbone of modern IoT systems, acting as the central nervous system that processes, stores, and analyzes the vast amounts of data generated by connected devices. They provide the scalable infrastructure and services necessary to handle the demands of IoT applications, enabling developers to focus on building innovative solutions rather than managing complex infrastructure. In essence, cloud platforms transform raw data into actionable insights, empowering businesses and individuals to make informed decisions and optimize their operations. They are the essential link between the physical world of connected devices and the digital world of data analysis and application development.

### Core Services Offered by Cloud Platforms for IoT

Cloud platforms offer a wide range of services specifically designed for IoT applications, including:

- **Device Management:** This service allows users to register, provision, and manage IoT devices at scale. It provides tools for device authentication, authorization, and remote configuration.
- **Data Ingestion and Storage:** Cloud platforms offer scalable storage solutions for handling the massive volumes of data generated by IoT devices. They provide data ingestion services for collecting data from various sources and storing it in

databases or data lakes.

- **Data Processing and Analytics**: Cloud platforms provide powerful analytics tools for processing and analyzing IoT data. These tools can be used to perform real-time data analysis, machine learning, and predictive analytics.
- **Security and Identity Management**: Cloud platforms offer robust security features to protect IoT data and devices. These features include encryption, authentication, authorization, and access control.
- **Application Development and Deployment**: Cloud platforms provide tools and services for developing and deploying IoT applications. These tools include SDKs, APIs, and development environments.

**Major Cloud Platform Providers and Their Offerings**

Several major cloud platform providers offer comprehensive IoT services, including:

**AWS IoT Core:** Amazon Web Services (AWS) provides a wide range of IoT services, including device management, data ingestion, data analytics, and security. AWS IoT Core is a fully managed service that allows users to connect, manage, and secure IoT devices at scale.

**Azure IoT Hub:** Microsoft Azure offers a comprehensive suite of IoT services, including device provisioning, data streaming, and analytics. Azure IoT Hub provides a secure and scalable platform for connecting and managing IoT devices.

**Google Cloud IoT Core (or related Google Services):** While Google Cloud IoT Core itself is being phased out, Google Cloud provides a robust set of services for IoT, including Pub/Sub for data ingestion, BigQuery for data analytics, and Cloud Functions for serverless computing. Google Cloud's offerings allow for the creation of robust IoT solutions.

**Other Platforms:** There are other very useful platforms, like IBM Watson IoT platform, and many others, that provide excellent services.

**Data Processing and Analytics in the Cloud**

Cloud platforms play a crucial role in processing and analyzing IoT data. They provide powerful analytics tools that can be used to extract valuable insights from the data. Real-time data analysis can be used to monitor device performance, detect anomalies, and trigger alerts. Machine learning algorithms can be used to identify patterns and trends in the data, enabling predictive maintenance and other advanced applications. Data visualization tools can be used to create dashboards and reports that provide a clear and concise view of the data. Edge computing, where processing is done at the device or gateway level, is also becoming increasingly important in IoT applications. Cloud platforms are vital in the storage of the processed data, and the further analysis of that data.

**Scalability, Reliability, and Security of Cloud Platforms**

Cloud platforms offer several key advantages for IoT applications, including scalability, reliability, and security. Scalability allows IoT systems to handle increasing volumes of data and devices. Reliability ensures that IoT applications are always available and responsive. Security features protect IoT data and devices from unauthorized access and cyberattacks. Cloud platforms also provide cost-effective solutions for IoT applications, eliminating the need for businesses to invest in expensive infrastructure. The ability to update and manage the IoT devices from the cloud platform is also a very important feature. The cloud also allows for easy integration with other systems.

## APPLICATIONS AND USER INTERFACES: INTERACTING WITH THE DATA

Applications and user interfaces are the crucial components that enable users to interact with IoT data and control connected devices. They provide the bridge between the complex world of data and the intuitive experience of the user. Without effective applications and user interfaces, the vast amounts of data generated by IoT devices would be meaningless. These interfaces transform raw data into actionable insights, enabling users to monitor device performance, control device behavior, and make informed decisions. They are the gateway to the IoT ecosystem, empowering users to harness the power of connected devices.

**Types of IoT Applications and User Interfaces**

IoT applications and user interfaces can take many forms, depending on the specific use case and user requirements. Common types include:

- **Mobile Apps:** Mobile apps provide a convenient way for users to interact with IoT devices and data on their smartphones and tablets.
- **Web Dashboards:** Web dashboards provide a centralized view of IoT data and device status, allowing users to monitor performance and control devices from a web browser.
- **Voice Interfaces:** Voice interfaces, such as Amazon Alexa and Google Assistant, allow users to control IoT devices using voice commands.
- **Augmented Reality (AR) and Virtual Reality (VR) Interfaces:** AR and VR interfaces provide immersive experiences that allow users to interact with IoT data and devices in a more intuitive way.
- **API's:** Application Programming Interfaces allow other applications to interact with the data that is being gathered.

**Key Considerations for Designing Effective User Interfaces**

Designing effective user interfaces for IoT applications requires careful consideration of several factors, including:

- **Usability:** User interfaces should be intuitive and easy to use, even for users with limited technical knowledge.
- **Accessibility:** User interfaces should be accessible to users with disabilities, such as visual or hearing impairments.
- **Security:** User interfaces should be secure and protect user data from unauthorized access.
- **Performance:** User interfaces should be responsive and provide real-time updates of IoT data.

- **Context Awareness:** User interfaces should be context-aware, providing relevant information and controls based on the user's location, time, and other factors.

### Data Visualization and Interaction Techniques

Data visualization plays a crucial role in making IoT data understandable and actionable. Common data visualization techniques include charts, graphs, and maps. Interaction techniques, such as touch gestures and voice commands, allow users to control IoT devices and navigate through data. User interfaces should provide clear and concise visualizations that highlight key insights and trends in the data. They should also provide intuitive interaction techniques that allow users to easily control devices and explore data. The user interface should be designed with the user in mind.

### The Future of IoT Applications and User Interfaces

The future of IoT applications and user interfaces is about creating more intelligent and personalized experiences. Artificial intelligence and machine learning will play a crucial role in enabling applications to adapt to user preferences and provide proactive recommendations. Natural language processing will enable more natural and intuitive voice interactions. Augmented reality and virtual reality will provide immersive experiences that allow users to interact with IoT data and devices in a more engaging way. The development of more intelligent user interfaces will be a key factor in the widespread adoption of IoT. The user experience will be the deciding factor in weather or not an IOT product is successful.

# FIVE

# COMMUNICATION PROTOCOLS IN IOT

In the intricate tapestry of the Internet of Things (IoT), where countless devices interact and exchange data, communication protocols serve as the fundamental language that facilitates this dialogue. These protocols are the unseen architects of connectivity, defining the rules and standards that govern how devices communicate with each other and with the broader network. Without them, the vast potential of IoT would remain unrealized, a cacophony of isolated devices unable to share information or coordinate actions. Just as human languages enable us to understand and interact with one another, communication protocols provide the framework for devices to understand and interact with their environment and with each other. This section is dedicated to unraveling the complexities of these essential protocols, exploring the diverse range of technologies that underpin the interconnected world of IoT. We will explore the different ways that devices communicate, and how these communications are made possible.

The landscape of IoT communication is diverse, encompassing a wide array of protocols designed to meet the unique requirements of various applications. From short-range, low-power protocols like Bluetooth and Zigbee, ideal for personal area networks and home automation, to long-range, wide-area protocols like LoRaWAN and cellular technologies, enabling global connectivity for remote monitoring and asset tracking, the choices are vast. We'll delve into the intricacies of each protocol, examining its strengths, weaknesses, and suitability for specific use cases. We'll explore how wireless protocols like Wi-Fi and Bluetooth enable seamless connectivity in indoor environments, while cellular technologies like 4G, 5G, and NB-IoT extend the reach of IoT to remote and challenging locations. We'll also examine the role of wired protocols, such as Ethernet and serial communication, which provide reliable and secure connections in industrial and critical infrastructure applications. Understanding this spectrum of communication protocols is essential for building robust and scalable IoT solutions that can address the diverse needs of a connected world. We'll cover the reasons why certain protocols are chosen over others, and what factors are taken into consideration.

Communication protocols are not merely about enabling data exchange; they are also about ensuring the reliability, security, and efficiency of IoT systems. Reliability ensures that data is transmitted accurately and consistently, even in challenging environments. Security protocols protect sensitive data from unauthorized access and cyberattacks, safeguarding the integrity of IoT networks. Efficiency is crucial for optimizing power consumption and minimizing network congestion, particularly in battery-powered devices and large-scale deployments. We'll explore how these protocols address these critical aspects, examining the mechanisms and techniques used to ensure robust and secure communication. The selection of the correct communication protocol can be the difference between a successful project, and a failed one. We will explore how to make the right choice, and what considerations should be taken before the selection is made. By understanding the intricacies of communication protocols, you'll gain a deeper appreciation for the essential role they play in enabling the transformative potential of the Internet of Things. This knowledge will empower you to design and implement IoT solutions that are not only functional but also reliable, secure, and efficient.

**WIRELESS PROTOCOLS**

Wireless communication protocols are the lifeblood of many IoT applications, enabling devices to connect and exchange data without the constraints of physical cables. Each protocol has its own unique characteristics, strengths, and weaknesses, making it suitable for specific use cases. Understanding these differences is crucial for choosing the right protocol for your IoT project. Wi-Fi, Bluetooth, Zigbee, and LoRaWAN represent a spectrum of wireless technologies, each designed to address different needs in terms of range, data rate, power consumption, and network topology. We will start by exploring each of these technologies, and then compare them.

**Wi-Fi and Bluetooth: Familiar Connectivity**

- **Wi-Fi (Wireless Fidelity):**

  - Based on the IEEE 802.11 standards, Wi-Fi is widely used for high-bandwidth applications, such as video streaming and internet browsing.
  - It offers relatively high data rates and a moderate range, making it suitable for indoor environments.
  - Wi-Fi is power-intensive, which limits its use in battery-powered IoT devices.
  - It is ideal for applications that require high data throughput and existing infrastructure, such as smart homes and industrial automation.

- **Bluetooth:**

  - Designed for short-range communication, Bluetooth is commonly used for connecting personal devices, such as smartphones, headphones, and wearables.
  - Bluetooth Low Energy (BLE) is a power-efficient variant that is well-suited for battery-powered IoT devices.

- Bluetooth offers a moderate data rate and a limited range, making it suitable for applications such as proximity sensing, device pairing, and data transfer.
- Bluetooth mesh networking extends the range of Bluetooth.

**Zigbee and LoRaWAN: Specialized IoT Connectivity**

- **Zigbee:**

  - Based on the IEEE 802.15.4 standard, Zigbee is a low-power, low-data-rate protocol designed for mesh networking.
  - It is commonly used in home automation, industrial control, and sensor networks.
  - Zigbee offers a moderate range and low power consumption, making it suitable for battery-powered devices in large networks.
  - Zigbee is designed for local area networks.

- **LoRaWAN (Long Range Wide Area Network):**

  - Designed for long-range, low-power communication, LoRaWAN is ideal for applications that require wide-area coverage and low data rates.
  - It is commonly used in smart city applications, such as environmental monitoring, asset tracking, and smart metering.
  - LoRaWAN offers a very long range and extremely low power consumption, making it suitable for battery-powered devices in remote locations.
  - LoRaWAN is designed for wide area networks.

**Comparing and Contrasting Wireless Protocols**

Choosing the right wireless protocol depends on the specific requirements of your IoT project. Key factors to consider include:

- **Range:** The distance over which devices need to communicate.
- **Data Rate:** The amount of data that needs to be transmitted.
- **Power Consumption:** The power requirements of the devices.
- **Network Topology:** The structure of the network (e.g., star, mesh).
- **Cost:** The cost of implementing and deploying the protocol.
- **Security:** The level of security required for the application.
- A table showing the comparison of the different wireless protocols is very useful.

## CELLULAR PROTOCOLS: 4G, 5G, NB-IOT

Cellular communication protocols provide a reliable and ubiquitous way to connect IoT devices to the internet. 4G, 5G, and NB-IoT represent a range of cellular technologies, each designed to address different needs in terms of data rate, latency, and power consumption. These technologies are very useful when Wi-Fi is not available, or when very long range is needed.

**4G and 5G: High-Bandwidth Cellular Connectivity)**

- **4G (Fourth Generation):**

  - 4G LTE (Long-Term Evolution) is a widely deployed cellular technology that offers high data rates and low latency.
  - It is suitable for IoT applications that require high bandwidth, such as video surveillance, connected vehicles, and industrial automation.
  - 4G is relatively power-intensive, which can limit its use in battery-powered IoT devices.

- **5G (Fifth Generation):**

  - 5G is the latest generation of cellular technology, offering even higher data rates, lower latency, and greater network capacity than 4G.

- It is ideal for applications that require ultra-low latency, such as autonomous vehicles, virtual reality, and industrial automation.
- 5G offers a range of frequency bands, including millimeter wave (mmWave), which provides very high data rates but a limited range.

### NB-IoT: Low-Power Cellular Connectivity

- **NB-IoT (Narrowband IoT):**

  - NB-IoT is a low-power, wide-area (LPWA) cellular technology designed for IoT applications that require long-range communication and low power consumption.
  - It is suitable for applications such as smart metering, asset tracking, and environmental monitoring.
  - NB-IoT offers a very long range and extremely low power consumption, making it ideal for battery-powered devices in remote locations.
  - NB-IoT is designed for applications that only require small amounts of data to be sent.

### Cellular Protocol Considerations

Choosing the right cellular protocol depends on the specific requirements of your IoT project. Key factors to consider include:

- **Data Rate:** The amount of data that needs to be transmitted.
- **Latency:** The delay in data transmission.
- **Power Consumption:** The power requirements of the devices.
- **Coverage:** The availability of cellular coverage in the deployment area.
- **Cost:** The cost of cellular data plans and hardware.
- **Security:** The level of security provided by the cellular network.
- Cellular protocols are very useful for applications that require global connectivity.

# WIRED PROTOCOLS: ETHERNET, SERIAL COMMUNICATION

Wired communication protocols provide a reliable and secure way to connect IoT devices in environments where wireless connectivity is not feasible or desirable. Ethernet and serial communication are two common wired protocols used in IoT applications.

### Ethernet:

- Based on the IEEE 802.3 standard, Ethernet is a widely used wired protocol for local area networks (LANs).
- It offers high data rates and low latency, making it suitable for applications that require high bandwidth and real-time communication.
- Ethernet is commonly used in industrial automation, building automation, and smart city infrastructure.
- Ethernet is very reliable.

### Serial Communication

- Serial communication is a simple and versatile protocol that transmits data one bit at a time over a single wire.
- Common serial communication standards include UART (Universal Asynchronous Receiver/Transmitter), SPI (Serial Peripheral Interface), and I2C (Inter-Integrated Circuit).
- Serial communication is commonly used for connecting sensors, actuators, and other peripheral devices to microcontrollers.
- Serial communication is very useful for short range communication between devices.

### Wired Protocol Considerations

Choosing the right wired protocol depends on the specific requirements of your IoT project. Key factors to consider include:

- **Data Rate:** The amount of data that needs to be transmitted.
- **Distance:** The distance over which devices need to communicate.
- **Complexity:** The complexity of implementing and deploying the protocol.
- **Cost:** The cost of hardware and cabling.
- **Reliability:** The reliability of the connection.
- Wired protocols are very useful in applications where security and reliability are

## CHOOSING THE RIGHT PROTOCOL FOR YOUR PROJECT

Selecting the appropriate communication protocol is a critical step in developing a successful IoT project. The choice depends on a variety of factors, including the application requirements, environmental conditions, and cost constraints.

**Key Factors in Protocol Selection**

**Application Requirements:**

- Data Rate: High-bandwidth applications (e.g., video streaming) require protocols like Wi-Fi or 4G/5G. Low-data-rate applications (e.g., sensor networks) can use protocols like Zigbee, LoRaWAN, or NB-IoT.
- Range: Wide-area applications require protocols like LoRaWAN or cellular. Local-area applications can use protocols like Wi-Fi, Bluetooth, or Zigbee.

# SIX

# IOT SECURITY AND PRIVACY

The Internet of Things (IoT), with its promise of seamless automation and data-driven insights, has ushered in an era of unprecedented connectivity. However, this interconnectedness comes with a significant caveat: the pervasive and often overlooked vulnerabilities that threaten the security and privacy of our digital and physical lives. In a world where everyday objects are becoming increasingly intelligent and interconnected, the potential for malicious actors to exploit weaknesses and compromise sensitive data is ever-present. From compromised smart home devices to large-scale industrial control systems, the consequences of security breaches and privacy violations can be devastating. Thus, the topic of IoT security and privacy is not merely a technical concern; it's a fundamental imperative for building a trustworthy and sustainable IoT ecosystem. We must acknowledge that the very nature of interconnectedness, while offering immense benefits, also creates a complex web of potential vulnerabilities. To truly harness the transformative power of IoT, we must first address the shadow side of connectivity, establishing robust security measures and ethical guidelines that protect both individuals and organizations from the potential risks. This is the foundation upon which trust is built, and without trust, the full potential of IoT will remain unrealized.

Unlike traditional IT systems, IoT devices are often deployed in diverse and unpredictable environments, making them susceptible to physical tampering and network vulnerabilities. Moreover, the vast amounts of data generated by these devices raise significant privacy concerns, requiring careful consideration of data collection, storage, and use practices. We must navigate the complexities of encryption, authentication, access control, and data governance, establishing robust security protocols that protect against cyberattacks and unauthorized access. Simultaneously, we must address the ethical implications of IoT data, ensuring that individuals' privacy rights are respected and that data is used responsibly and transparently. This section will delve into the intricacies of IoT security and privacy, exploring the various threats and vulnerabilities that exist, and examining the best practices for mitigating these risks. It will highlight the importance of building security into IoT systems from the design phase, and the necessity of establishing clear ethical guidelines for data collection and use. It will also examine the regulations that are in place, and the responsibilities of the creators of IoT products. By fostering a culture of security and privacy, we can build trust in IoT technologies and unlock their full potential to create a more connected, efficient, and secure world.

## UNDERSTANDING SECURITY RISKS IN IOT

The rapid proliferation of IoT devices has created a vast and interconnected landscape, but this connectivity also introduces significant security risks. Unlike traditional IT systems, IoT devices are often resource-constrained, deployed in diverse environments, and managed by individuals or organizations with varying levels of security expertise. This makes them attractive targets for cyberattacks. Understanding the specific security risks associated with IoT is essential for mitigating potential threats and protecting sensitive data. The increased attack surface is one of the biggest challenges.

**Common Security Threats in IoT**
**Device Vulnerabilities:**

- Many IoT devices have inherent vulnerabilities due to weak default passwords, outdated firmware, or insecure software.
- These vulnerabilities can be exploited by attackers to gain unauthorized access to devices and networks.
- Lack of proper security updates from manufacturers exacerbates these issues.

## Network Attacks:

- IoT networks can be targeted by various network attacks, such as denial-of-service (DoS) attacks, man-in-the-middle (MitM) attacks, and botnet attacks.
- DoS attacks can disrupt the availability of IoT services, while MitM attacks can intercept and manipulate data.
- Botnets made from compromised IOT devices, are a large threat.

## Data Breaches:

- IoT devices often collect and transmit sensitive data, such as personal information, health data, and financial data.
- Data breaches can occur due to weak encryption, insecure storage, or unauthorized access to data.
- Data stored in cloud services is also vulnerable.

## Physical Attacks:

- IoT devices deployed in public or remote locations can be vulnerable to physical tampering or theft.
- Physical attacks can compromise the integrity of devices and data.
- Easy access to IOT devices, can be a large security risk.

## Supply Chain Attacks:

- Attacks can happen during the manufacturing process.
- Compromised components can be installed into IOT devices, before they are sold.

## The Impact of Security Breaches in IoT

The consequences of security breaches in IoT can be severe, including:

- **Financial Losses**: Businesses can suffer financial losses due to data breaches, service disruptions, and reputational damage.
- **Privacy Violations**: Individuals can experience privacy violations due to the unauthorized collection and use of their personal data.
- **Safety Risks**: Security breaches in critical infrastructure, such as healthcare or transportation, can pose safety risks to individuals and communities.
- **Operational Disruptions**: Attacks can disrupt operations in industrial settings, leading to production delays and financial losses.
- **Loss of trust**: When a company has a security breach, the trust of their customers is damaged.

## The Unique Challenges of IoT Security

IoT security presents unique challenges due to the diversity of devices, the scale of deployments, and the resource constraints of many devices.

- **Heterogeneity**: IoT devices have diverse hardware and software platforms, making it difficult to implement uniform security measures.
- **Scalability**: IoT deployments can involve thousands or even millions of devices, making it challenging to manage security at scale.
- **Resource Constraints**: Many IoT devices have limited processing power, memory, and battery life, making it difficult to

implement complex security mechanisms.

- **Lack of Standardization:** The lack of standardized security protocols and practices makes it difficult to ensure interoperability and security across different IoT ecosystems.
- **Lifespan of devices:** Many IOT devices have a long lifespan, and may outlive the support of the manufacturer.

### The Evolving Threat Landscape

The threat landscape for IoT is constantly evolving, with new attack vectors and vulnerabilities emerging regularly. It is essential to stay informed about the latest security threats and best practices. Ongoing monitoring, vulnerability assessments, and security updates are crucial for maintaining the security of IoT systems. The security of IOT devices, must be a priority from the very beginning of the design process.

## IMPLEMENTING SECURITY BEST PRACTICES: ENCRYPTION, AUTHENTICATION, ACCESS CONTROL

Implementing robust security best practices is essential for protecting IoT devices and data from cyberattacks. Encryption, authentication, and access control are fundamental security mechanisms that should be implemented in all IoT systems. These practices are the first line of defence against malicious actors.

- **Data Encryption:**

  - Encryption is the process of converting data into an unreadable format, protecting it from unauthorized access.
  - Data should be encrypted both in transit and at rest.
  - Transport Layer Security (TLS) and Secure Sockets Layer (SSL) are commonly used protocols for encrypting data in transit.
  - Advanced Encryption Standard (AES) is a widely used algorithm for encrypting data at rest.

- **Key Management:**

- Secure key management is essential for ensuring the effectiveness of encryption.
- Keys should be securely generated, stored, and distributed.
- Hardware Security Modules (HSMs) can be used to protect cryptographic keys.

## AUTHENTICATION

- **Device Authentication:**

  - Device authentication is the process of verifying the identity of IoT devices.
  - Mutual authentication, where both devices verify each other's identities, is recommended.
  - Digital certificates and public key infrastructure (PKI) can be used for device authentication.

- **User Authentication:**

  - User authentication is the process of verifying the identity of users accessing IoT systems.
  - Strong passwords, multi-factor authentication (MFA), and biometric authentication should be used.
  - Role based access control should also be used.

**Access Control: Restricting Access to Resources**

- **Role-Based Access Control (RBAC):**

  - RBAC is a mechanism for restricting access to resources based on the roles of users and devices.
  - RBAC ensures that users and devices only have access to the resources they need.

- **Least Privilege Principle:**

- The least privilege principle states that users and devices should only have the minimum necessary privileges to perform their tasks.
- This principle minimizes the potential impact of security breaches.

- **Network Segmentation:**

  - Segmenting the network, limits the spread of malware.
  - This limits the amount of damage that can be done, from a single compromised device.

**Security Updates and Patch Management**

- **Firmware and Software Updates:**

  - Regular firmware and software updates are essential for patching vulnerabilities and maintaining the security of IoT devices.
  - Manufacturers should provide timely security updates and support for their devices.

- **Patch Management:**

  - Organizations should implement a patch management process to ensure that security updates are applied promptly.
  - Automated patch management tools can help streamline this process.
  - Keeping IOT devices up to date, is a critical part of security.
  - Security must be considered at every stage of the devices lifecycle.

**DATA PRIVACY AND ETHICAL CONSIDERATIONS**

IoT devices collect and process vast amounts of personal data, raising significant privacy concerns. Data privacy is the right of individuals to control the collection, use, and disclosure of their personal information. Ethical considerations play a crucial role in ensuring that IoT technologies are used responsibly and in a way that respects individual privacy.

**Data Collection and Usage in IoT**

**Types of Data Collected:** IoT devices collect a wide range of data, including location data, health data, usage data, and environmental data. This data can be used to create detailed profiles of individuals and their activities.

**Data Usage:** Data collected by IoT devices can be used for various purposes, such as personalization, analytics, and marketing. It is important to ensure that data is used in a transparent and ethical manner. Data should only be collected when needed.

**Privacy Risks and Challenges**

- **Lack of Transparency:**

  - Many IoT devices collect data without the explicit consent or knowledge of users.
  - This lack of transparency can lead to privacy violations.

- **Data Aggregation and Profiling:**

  - Data from multiple IoT devices can be aggregated to create detailed profiles of individuals.
  - This profiling can be used for targeted advertising, surveillance, or other purposes.

- **Data Sharing and Third Parties:**

  - Data collected by IoT devices may be shared with third parties, such as advertisers or data brokers.
  - Users may not have control over how their data is used by these third parties.

- **Data Security Breaches:**

  - As stated earlier, data breaches can expose sensitive personal information.
  - The consequences of a data breach, can be severe

## Ethical Guidelines and Best Practices

- **Develop Ethical Guidelines:** Organizations should develop ethical guidelines for the collection, storage, and use of IoT data.
- **Conduct Privacy Impact Assessments (PIAs):** PIAs can help identify and mitigate privacy risks associated with IoT projects.
- **Implement Privacy-Enhancing Technologies (PETs):** PETs can help protect data privacy by anonymizing, pseudonymizing, and aggregating data.
- **Promote Transparency and Accountability:** Organizations should be transparent about how they collect and use IoT data, and they should be accountable for their actions.
- **Engage with Stakeholders:** Organizations should engage with stakeholders, such as users, regulators, and civil society organizations, to address privacy and ethical concerns.

## The Future of IoT Privacy and Ethics

- **Privacy by Design and Default:** Privacy should be integrated into the design of IoT systems from the outset.
- **Data Governance Frameworks:** Data governance frameworks should be established to ensure that IoT data is managed responsibly.
- **Ethical AI and Machine Learning:** Ethical principles should be incorporated into the development and deployment of AI and machine learning algorithms used in IoT systems.
- **International Collaboration:** International collaboration is essential for developing global standards and regulations for IoT privacy and ethics.

- **Public Awareness and Education:** Public awareness and education are essential for promoting responsible data practices and fostering trust in IoT technologies.
- The creation of a culture of privacy and ethics is essential.

# SEVEN

# GETTING STARTED WITH IOT DEVELOPMENT

The foundational concepts of the Internet of Things (IoT), from its architectural underpinnings to the critical considerations of security and privacy, it's time to embark on a journey from theoretical understanding to practical application. This second part of our guide, "Getting Started with IoT Development," is dedicated to empowering you with the hands-on skills necessary to bring your IoT ideas to life. We're moving beyond the abstract and diving into the concrete, transitioning from passive observers to active creators. This is where the real excitement begins, where you'll transform your newfound knowledge into tangible projects, building your own connected devices and experiencing the thrill of seeing your creations interact with the world around them. This section is designed to be your launchpad, providing you with the essential tools, techniques, and guidance to embark on your IoT development adventure. We will be building projects, and learning by doing.

The world of IoT development offers a diverse array of platforms and tools, each with its own strengths and characteristics.We'll guide you through the process of selecting the right platform for your needs, whether it's the beginner-friendly Arduino, the powerful Raspberry Pi, or the versatile ESP32. We'll demystify the setup process, providing step-by-step instructions for installing the necessary software and configuring your development environment. But it's not just about setting up tools; it's about building your skills. We'll introduce you to the fundamental programming concepts that underpin IoT development, from variables and loops to functions and data structures. You'll learn how to interface with sensors and actuators, the building blocks of any IoT project, enabling you to collect data from the environment and control physical devices. This practical approach will empower you to move beyond theoretical understanding and embrace the hands-on experience of building real-world IoT solutions. We will begin with basic examples, and move to more advanced projects.

The best way to learn IoT development is by doing. We'll guide you through the process of building your first IoT projects, starting with simple applications like a smart home temperature monitoring system and a remote-controlled LED. As you progress, you'll tackle more complex projects, such as a motion-activated security system, applying your newfound skills to create increasingly sophisticated solutions. We'll also cover cloud platform integrations, and mobile app integration, to further expand your skillset. This journey is about embracing the IoT maker spirit, experimenting, iterating, and learning from your experiences. We encourage you to tinker, explore, and let your creativity guide you as you build your own connected devices. This section is designed to be a starting point, to give you the foundation you need to continue to learn and grow as an IoT developer. We will give you the tools, and the knowledge, to continue to explore on your own. By the end of this section, you'll have the confidence and skills to tackle your own IoT projects, transforming your ideas into reality and contributing to the ever-expanding world of connected things.

# EIGHT

# CHOOSING YOUR DEVELOPMENT PLATFORM

In the realm of Internet of Things (IoT) development, the choice of your platform is akin to an architect selecting the foundation upon which a building will stand. It dictates the structural integrity, the scope of possibilities, and the overall success of your project. This pivotal decision, "Choosing Your Development Platform," is not merely a matter of picking a piece of hardware or software; it's about aligning your vision with the right tools to bring it to fruition. In the vast landscape of IoT, where every project possesses unique requirements and constraints, the platform you select will significantly influence the capabilities, limitations, and overall development experience. It's the starting point for your creative journey, the bedrock upon which you'll build your connected creations. This introduction aims to illuminate the importance of this decision, guiding you through the considerations and choices that will shape your IoT endeavors. Understanding your platform is essential to the success of your project.

The process of choosing a development platform is not a one-size-fits-all endeavor. It requires a thorough understanding of your project's specific needs and a clear grasp of the diverse platform landscape. Before diving into the technical specifications of each platform, it's crucial to define your project's requirements, outlining the functionality, processing power, connectivity options, and power consumption constraints. Consider the complexity of your application, the level of real-time performance required, and the anticipated scale of your project. Once you have a clear understanding of your project's needs, you can begin to explore the various platforms available, each with its own strengths and characteristics. We'll delve into the beginner-friendly world of Arduino, the powerful capabilities of the Raspberry Pi, the integrated connectivity of the ESP32, and the specialized offerings of other platforms like NodeMCU and BeagleBone. We will explain how each of these platforms work, and what they are best suited for. By carefully evaluating your project requirements and comparing the features of each platform, you can make an informed decision that sets you on the path to success.

Choosing a development platform is not solely about hardware specifications; it's also about the ecosystem that surrounds it. The availability of a strong community, comprehensive documentation, and readily accessible resources can significantly impact your development experience. A vibrant community can provide support, answer questions, and share knowledge, while good documentation and example projects can help you get started quickly and overcome challenges. Consider the availability of libraries and tools that can simplify your development process. The platform you choose will become your primary tool, so ensuring that you have the resources to use it is essential. Furthermore, the selection of the platform sets the tone for your entire development journey. It's the tool that will be used to bring your ideas to life. This chapter will give you the tools to make that decision. The journey of IoT development is one of continuous learning and exploration. By choosing the right platform, you're not just selecting a piece of hardware; you're embarking on a path of discovery, innovation, and creation. This section will empower you to make an informed decision, setting you on the path to building your own connected world.

## THE FOUNDATION OF YOUR IOT JOURNEY

Selecting the right development platform is a crucial first step in any IoT project. The platform you choose will determine the capabilities and limitations of your project, as well as the ease of development and deployment. There's no one-size-fits-all solution; the best platform depends on your specific needs, skills, and budget. This section will guide you through the process of choosing the right platform, highlighting the key factors to consider and providing an overview of popular options. The development platform is the core of the project, and the tool that you will be using to bring your ideas to life.

**Key Factors to Consider When Choosing a Platform**

- **Project Requirements:**

  - **Processing Power:** How much processing power is required for your application?
  - **Connectivity:** What type of connectivity is needed (Wi-Fi, Bluetooth, cellular, etc.)?
  - **Input/Output (I/O) Capabilities:** How many sensors and actuators will your project use?
  - **Power Consumption:** Is power consumption a critical factor for your application?
  - **Real-Time Performance:** Does your application require real-time performance?

- **Development Environment:**

  - **Programming Language:** What programming languages are supported by the platform?
  - **Integrated Development Environment (IDE):** Is there a user-friendly IDE available?

- **Libraries and Tools:** Are there sufficient libraries and tools available for your project?
- **Community Support:** Is there a large and active community of developers?

- **Cost:**

  - **Hardware Costs:** The cost of the development board and other hardware components.
  - **Software Costs:** The cost of development tools and libraries.
  - **Deployment Costs:** The cost of deploying and maintaining the project.

- **Ease of Use:**

  - **Learning Curve:** How steep is the learning curve for the platform?
  - **Documentation:** Is there good documentation available?
  - **Example Projects:** Are there example projects available to get started?

- **Scalability:**

  - Can the platform scale as your project grows?
  - Can the platform handle increasing amounts of data and devices?

Before diving into specific platforms, it's essential to define your project requirements. Start by outlining the functionality of your project, identifying the sensors and actuators you'll need, and determining the connectivity requirements. Consider the processing power required for your application, as well as the power consumption constraints. Think about the development environment you prefer, including the programming language and IDE. Assess your budget and consider the long-term scalability of your project. By clearly defining your project requirements, you'll be better equipped to choose the right development platform.

A strong community and readily available resources can significantly impact your development experience. A large and active community can provide support, answer questions, and share knowledge. Good documentation and example projects can help you get started quickly and overcome challenges. Consider the availability of libraries and tools that can simplify your development process. The community can be a great help when you encounter problems.

**Making the Final Decision**

Choosing the right development platform is a personal decision that depends on your specific needs and preferences. Don't be afraid to experiment with different platforms and find the one that best suits you. Consider starting with a beginner-friendly platform like Arduino and gradually moving to more advanced platforms like Raspberry Pi or ESP32 as your skills and experience grow. The selection of the platform will set the tone for the entire project.

## ARDUINO: THE BEGINNER-FRIENDLY PLATFORM

**Simplicity and Accessibility**

Arduino is a popular open-source electronics platform that is known for its simplicity, accessibility, and ease of use. It's an ideal platform for beginners and hobbyists who are new to electronics and programming. Arduino consists of a physical programmable circuit board (often referred to as a microcontroller) and a software development environment (IDE) that runs on your computer. The Arduino IDE uses a simplified version of C++, making it easy to learn and use. Arduino is designed to make electronics accessible to everyone, regardless of their technical background.

**Key Features and Benefits of Arduino**

- **Ease of Use:** Arduino's user-friendly IDE and simplified programming language make it easy to get started.
- **Large Community:** Arduino has a large and active community that provides support, tutorials, and example projects.

- **Wide Range of Boards:** Arduino offers a wide range of boards to suit different needs and applications.
- **Extensive Libraries:** Arduino has a vast library of pre-written code that simplifies common tasks.
- **Low Cost:** Arduino boards are relatively inexpensive, making them accessible to a wide range of users.
- **Cross-Platform IDE:** The Arduino IDE runs on Windows, macOS, and Linux.
- **Open-Source:** Arduino is open-source, which means that the hardware and software are freely available.

**Arduino Applications and Use Cases**

Arduino is used in a wide range of applications, including:

- **Home Automation:** Controlling lights, appliances, and other devices in the home.
- **Robotics:** Building robots and other automated machines.
- **Sensor Networks:** Collecting data from sensors and transmitting it to a central location.
- **Art and Design:** Creating interactive art installations and design prototypes.
- **Education:** Teaching electronics and programming to students of all ages.
- **Prototyping:** Creating prototypes of electronic devices.

To get started with Arduino, you'll need an Arduino board, a USB cable, and a computer. You can download the Arduino IDE from the official Arduino website. Once you have the IDE installed, you can connect your Arduino board to your computer and start writing code. Arduino has many tutorials online to help a new user get started.

While Arduino is a great platform for beginners, it has some limitations. Arduino boards have limited processing power and memory, which can restrict the complexity of your projects. Arduino is not ideal for applications that require real-time performance or high-bandwidth communication. However, for many IoT projects, Arduino provides a simple and cost-effective solution.

**Raspberry Pi: The Powerful Microcomputer**

The Raspberry Pi is a small, single-board computer that offers a powerful and versatile platform for IoT development. Unlike Arduino, which is a microcontroller, the Raspberry Pi is a full-fledged computer that runs a Linux-based operating system. This gives it significantly more processing power, memory, and connectivity options than Arduino. The Raspberry Pi is ideal for projects that require complex processing, networking, and multimedia capabilities.

**Key Features and Benefits of Raspberry Pi**

- **Powerful Processor:** The Raspberry Pi has a powerful processor that can handle complex tasks.
- **Plenty of Memory:** The Raspberry Pi has ample memory for running applications and storing data.
- **Multiple Connectivity Options:** The Raspberry Pi has a wide range of connectivity options, including Wi-Fi, Ethernet, and Bluetooth.
- **Full-Fledged Operating System:** The Raspberry Pi runs a Linux-based operating system, which provides access to a vast library of software and tools.
- **GPIO Pins:** The Raspberry Pi has GPIO (General Purpose Input/Output) pins that can be used to connect sensors and actuators.
- **Large Community:** The Raspberry Pi has a large and active community that provides support, tutorials, and example projects.
- **Multimedia Capabilities:** The Raspberry Pi has multimedia capabilities, including HDMI output and audio output.

**Raspberry Pi Applications and Use Cases**

The Raspberry Pi is used in a wide range of applications, including:

- **Home Automation:** Controlling lights, appliances, and other devices in the home.
- **Media Centers:** Building media centers for streaming video and audio.
- **Web Servers:** Hosting websites and web applications.
- **Robotics:** Building robots and other automated machines.
- **IoT Gateways:** Acting as gateways for connecting IoT devices to the cloud.
- **Edge Computing:** Performing data processing at the edge of the network.

To get started with Raspberry Pi, you'll need a Raspberry Pi board, a microSD card, a power supply, a monitor, a keyboard, and a mouse. You can download the Raspberry Pi OS from the official Raspberry Pi website. Once you have the OS installed on the microSD card, you can insert it into the Raspberry Pi and boot it up. The Raspberry Pi community has many online tutorials to help new users. While the Raspberry Pi is a powerful platform, it has some limitations. It consumes more power than Arduino, which can be a concern for battery-powered applications. The Raspberry Pi's Linux-based operating system can be more complex to learn than Arduino's simplified programming language.

# NINE

# SETTING UP YOUR DEVELOPMENT ENVIRONMENT

Before you can bring your IoT ideas to life, you need a well-equipped workshop – not one of physical tools and materials, but a digital one. "Setting Up Your Development Environment" is the essential first step in your journey as an IoT developer. It's about creating the digital space where you'll write code, test circuits, and ultimately transform your concepts into tangible, connected devices. Just as a carpenter prepares their workspace with tools and materials, you'll prepare your computer with the necessary software, libraries, and configurations. This digital workshop will become your creative hub, the place where you'll translate your ideas into code, interact with your hardware, and debug your projects. This step is not merely about installing software; it's about building a foundation for your IoT development journey, creating a seamless and efficient workflow that allows you to focus on the creative process. Without a properly configured development environment, you will find yourself struggling to accomplish even the most basic tasks.

Setting up your development environment involves more than just downloading a few programs. It's about understanding the specific requirements of your chosen platform, configuring your software to work seamlessly with your hardware, and ensuring that you have all the necessary tools at your fingertips. We'll guide you through the process of installing the Integrated Development Environments (IDEs) specific to your chosen platforms, such as the Arduino IDE, or Raspberry Pi OS. We'll show you how to install the necessary libraries, the pre-written code that simplifies common tasks and expands the capabilities of your development environment. We'll cover the basics of the programming language that you will be using, and how to write basic code. We'll also cover how to test that the environment is working correctly, by writing basic code, and uploading it to the hardware. We'll address the essential steps for configuring your hardware, ensuring that it's properly connected and recognized by your computer. This groundwork is essential for a smooth and productive development experience. A well-configured environment minimizes frustration, allowing you to focus on the creative aspects of your project. This section is not just about technical steps; it's about empowering you to take control of your development process, creating a digital workspace that fosters innovation and creativity.

## THE FOUNDATION OF YOUR IOT WORKFLOW

Setting up your development environment is the crucial first step in any IoT project. It's the digital workshop where you'll write code, interact with hardware, and bring your ideas to life. A well-configured environment streamlines the development process, allowing you to focus on creativity rather than troubleshooting. This section will guide you through the essential steps, ensuring you have a smooth and efficient workflow. We'll cover the installation of necessary software, the setup of your chosen platform, and the essential programming concepts you'll need. The development environment is the tool that you will be using to create your project, and therefore is very important.

### Understanding the Components of a Development Environment

A typical IoT development environment consists of several key components:

- **Integrated Development Environment (IDE):** This is the software application where you write, compile, and debug your code.
- **Compiler:** This translates your code into machine-readable instructions that the microcontroller or microcomputer can execute.
- **Libraries:** These are pre-written code modules that provide functions and tools for common tasks, such as sensor interfacing and network communication.
- **Drivers:** These software components enable your computer to communicate with the development board.
- **Operating System (OS) (for platforms like Raspberry Pi):** The OS provides the foundation for running applications and managing hardware resources.
- **Hardware:** The physical development board you'll be working with.

**Importance of a Well-Configured Environment**

A well-configured development environment offers several advantages:

- Streamlined workflows and readily available tools save time and effort.
- Properly installed libraries and drivers minimize compatibility issues and errors.
- Effective debugging tools help identify and resolve issues quickly.
- A well-organized environment fosters a more enjoyable and effective learning experience.
- Having a consistent environment across multiple projects reduces setup time, and helps with debugging.

**Step-by-Step Approach to Setup**

We'll take a step-by-step approach to setting up your development environment, covering each platform in detail. This will include:

- Downloading and installing the necessary software.
- Configuring the IDE for your chosen platform.
- Installing required libraries and drivers.
- Testing the environment to ensure it's working correctly.
- Testing that the hardware is communicating with the software.

**(Page 5: Maintaining and Troubleshooting Your Environment)**

Maintaining your development environment is crucial for long-term productivity. This includes:

- Keeping software and libraries up to date.
- Regularly backing up your projects and configurations.
- Troubleshooting common issues, such as driver conflicts and software errors.
- Knowing how to find the answers to questions that arise.
- Knowing how to use the documentation that is provided.

**INSTALLING THE ARDUINO IDE**

The Arduino IDE (Integrated Development Environment) is the software application you'll use to write, compile, and upload code to your Arduino board. Its user-friendly interface and simplified programming language make it an ideal starting point for beginners. This section will guide you through the process of installing and configuring the Arduino IDE.

**Downloading and Installing the Arduino IDE**

- Visit the official Arduino website (arduino.cc) and navigate to the "Software" section.
- Download the appropriate version of the IDE for your operating system (Windows, macOS, or Linux).

- Run the installer and follow the on-screen instructions.
- Choose the default installation options for a standard setup.

**Configuring the Arduino IDE**

- Once the IDE is installed, connect your Arduino board to your computer using a USB cable.
- Open the Arduino IDE and navigate to "Tools" > "Board" and select your Arduino board model.
- Navigate to "Tools" > "Port" and select the serial port that your Arduino board is connected to.
- Verify that the correct board and port are selected.

**Writing Your First Arduino Sketch**

- Open a new sketch (code file) in the Arduino IDE.
- Write a simple "Blink" sketch that turns an LED on and off.
- Verify and upload the sketch to your Arduino board.
- Observe the LED blinking on your Arduino board.
- The "Blink" sketch is the "Hello world" of the Arduino world.

**Exploring the Arduino IDE Interface**

- Familiarize yourself with the Arduino IDE interface, including the code editor, serial monitor, and toolbar.
- Explore the various menus and options available in the IDE.
- Learn how to use the serial monitor to display data from your Arduino board.
- Learn how to use the library manager to install new libraries.
- Learn how to use the examples that are provided with the IDE.

**SETTING UP RASPBERRY PI OS**

Raspberry Pi OS (formerly Raspbian) is the official operating system for the Raspberry Pi. It provides a Linux-based environment for running applications, managing hardware, and developing IoT projects. This section will guide you through the process of installing and configuring Raspberry Pi OS.

**Downloading and Installing Raspberry Pi OS**

- Visit the official Raspberry Pi website (raspberrypi.org) and navigate to the "Software" section.
- Download the Raspberry Pi Imager tool.
- Insert a microSD card into your computer.
- Open the Raspberry Pi Imager tool and select the Raspberry Pi OS image.
- Select your microSD card as the target device.
- Click "Write" to install the OS image to the microSD card.

**Booting Up Raspberry Pi OS**

- Insert the microSD card into your Raspberry Pi.
- Connect a monitor, keyboard, and mouse to your Raspberry Pi.
- Connect a power supply to your Raspberry Pi to boot it up.
- Follow the on-screen instructions to complete the initial setup.

**Configuring Raspberry Pi OS**

- Connect your Raspberry Pi to a Wi-Fi network.
- Enable SSH (Secure Shell) to remotely access your Raspberry Pi.
- Update and upgrade the operating system.
- Install necessary software and libraries.
- Change the default password.

**Exploring the Raspberry Pi OS Environment**

- Familiarize yourself with the Raspberry Pi OS desktop environment.
- Explore the various applications and tools available.
- Learn how to use the command line interface.
- Learn how to use the built in python editor.

- Learn how to use the built in web browser.

## INSTALLING ESP32 LIBRARIES

ESP32 libraries provide pre-written code modules that simplify common tasks and extend the functionality of the ESP32 microcontroller. This section will guide you through the process of installing and using ESP32 libraries.

### Installing ESP32 Libraries Using the Arduino IDE Library Manager

- Open the Arduino IDE and navigate to "Tools" > "Manage Libraries...".
- Search for the library you want to install.
- Click "Install" to install the library.

### Installing ESP32 Libraries Manually

- Download the library from a repository (e.g., GitHub).
- Unzip the library files.
- Copy the library folder to the "libraries" folder in your Arduino sketchbook directory.

### Using ESP32 Libraries in Your Code

- Include the library in your code using the #include directive.
- Use the functions and classes provided by the library.

### Common ESP32 Libraries

- WiFi.h: For Wi-Fi communication.
- BluetoothSerial.h: For Bluetooth serial communication.
- PubSubClient.h: For MQTT communication.
- Wire.h: For I2C communication.
- SPI.h: For SPI communication.
- Many other libraries are available.

# TEN

# WORKING WITH SENSORS AND ACTUATORS

Sensors and actuators are the essential building blocks of any IoT system, acting as the bridge between the physical and digital worlds. Sensors gather data from the environment, converting physical phenomena into electrical signals that can be processed by microcontrollers and microcomputers. Actuators, on the other hand, take digital signals from the processing unit and translate them into physical actions, controlling devices and influencing the environment. Understanding how to work with sensors and actuators is fundamental to building effective and interactive IoT applications. They are the tools that allow your IoT projects to sense and interact with the real world.

Sensors are the eyes and ears of an IoT system. They measure various physical parameters, such as temperature, humidity, light, motion, pressure, and more. The data collected by sensors is then transmitted to a processing unit, where it can be analyzed and used to make decisions. Sensors can be analog or digital. Analog sensors produce a continuous voltage or current signal that is proportional to the measured parameter. Digital sensors produce a discrete digital signal that represents the measured parameter. The choice of sensor depends on the specific application and the type of data that needs to be collected. Sensors are what give your IoT project the ability to sense the world around it.

Actuators are the hands and feet of an IoT system. They take digital signals from the processing unit and convert them into physical actions. Common actuators include LEDs, motors, relays, and solenoids. LEDs are used to provide visual feedback and illumination. Motors are used to control the movement of mechanical devices. Relays are used to switch high-voltage circuits. Solenoids are used to control the flow of fluids and gases. The choice of actuator depends on the specific application and the type of action that needs to be performed. Actuators are what allow your IoT project to interact with the world around it.

Interfacing sensors and actuators with development boards like Arduino, Raspberry Pi, or ESP32 involves connecting them to the board's input/output (I/O) pins. Analog sensors are typically connected to analog input pins, while digital sensors are connected to digital input pins. Actuators are typically connected to digital output pins. The specific connections depend on the type of sensor or actuator and the development board being used. It is very important to consult the data sheet of the sensor or actuator before connecting it. Many sensors and actuators require external power supplies, or additional circuitry to function properly.

Once sensors and actuators are connected to the development board, you can write code to read data from sensors and control actuators. Reading data from sensors involves reading the analog or digital signals from the sensor's output pins. Controlling actuators involves sending digital signals to the actuator's input pins. The code for reading and controlling data depends on the programming language and the development board being used. Libraries are often available to simplify the process of reading and controlling data. It is important to calibrate sensors, and to test actuators before deploying them in a real world application.

## COMMON SENSORS: TEMPERATURE, HUMIDITY, LIGHT, MOTION (5 PAGES)

Common sensors like temperature, humidity, light, and motion are used in a wide range of IoT applications. They provide essential data about the environment, enabling IoT systems to monitor and control various parameters. These sensors are relatively inexpensive and easy to interface with development boards, making them ideal for beginners and hobbyists.

Temperature sensors measure the temperature of the environment. Common temperature sensors include thermistors, thermocouples, and LM35 sensors. Thermistors are resistors whose resistance changes with temperature. Thermocouples are made from two different metals that produce a voltage proportional to the temperature difference. LM35 sensors produce a voltage output that is directly proportional to the temperature. Temperature sensors are used in applications such as home automation, industrial control, and environmental monitoring.

Humidity sensors measure the relative humidity of the environment. Common humidity sensors include capacitive humidity sensors and resistive humidity sensors. Capacitive humidity sensors measure the change in capacitance of a dielectric material as the humidity changes. Resistive humidity sensors measure the change in resistance of a material as the humidity changes. Humidity sensors are used in applications such as home automation, agriculture, and weather monitoring.

Light sensors measure the intensity of light. Common light sensors include photoresistors and photodiodes. Photoresistors are resistors whose resistance changes with light intensity. Photodiodes produce a current proportional to the light intensity. Light sensors are used in applications such as home automation, security systems, and robotics.

Motion sensors detect the presence of motion. Common motion sensors include passive infrared (PIR) sensors and ultrasonic sensors. PIR sensors detect changes in infrared radiation caused by the movement of warm objects. Ultrasonic sensors emit ultrasonic sound waves and detect the reflected waves. Motion sensors are used in applications such as security systems, home automation, and robotics.

## COMMON ACTUATORS

Common actuators like LEDs, motors, and relays are used in a wide range of IoT applications. They provide essential control over physical devices and processes, enabling IoT systems to interact with the environment. These actuators are relatively inexpensive and easy to interface with development boards, making them ideal for beginners and hobbyists.

### LEDs (Light Emitting Diodes)

LEDs are semiconductor devices that emit light when an electric current passes through them. They are [1] used for visual feedback, illumination, and signaling. LEDs are available in a wide range of colors, sizes, and brightness levels. They are commonly used in applications such as home automation, robotics, and signage.

Motors are electromechanical devices that convert electrical energy into mechanical motion. They are used to control the movement of mechanical devices, such as robots, fans, and pumps. Motors are available in a wide range of types, including DC motors, stepper motors, and servo motors. DC motors rotate continuously when a voltage is applied. Stepper motors rotate in precise steps. Servo motors rotate to a specific angle. Motors are used in applications such as robotics, industrial automation, and home appliances.

### Relays

Relays are electromechanical switches that are used to control high-voltage circuits. They are used to switch high-power devices, such as lights, motors, and appliances. Relays are available in a wide range of types, including electromechanical relays and solid-state relays. Electromechanical relays use an electromagnet to switch the contacts. Solid-state relays use semiconductor devices to switch the contacts. Relays are used in applications such as industrial control, home automation, and automotive systems.

### Considerations for Actuator Selection

When selecting actuators for an IoT project, it is important to consider the following factors:

- **Voltage and Current Requirements:** The voltage and current requirements of the actuator must be compatible with the development board and power supply.
- **Type of Motion or Action:** The type of motion or action required by the application will determine the type of actuator needed.
- **Speed and Torque:** The speed and torque requirements of the application will determine the size and type of motor needed.
- **Switching Capacity:** The switching capacity of the relay must be sufficient to handle the load current.
- **Cost and Availability:** The cost and availability of the actuator should be considered.

## INTERFACING SENSORS AND ACTUATORS WITH YOUR DEVELOPMENT BOARD

**Connecting the Physical and Digital :** Interfacing sensors and actuators with your development board is the process of connecting them to the board's input/output (I/O) pins. This allows the development board to read data from sensors and control actuators. The specific connections depend on the type of sensor or actuator and the development board being used.

**Connecting Sensors:** Analog sensors are typically connected to analog input pins. Digital sensors are connected to digital input pins. The connections are made using wires or jumper cables. It is important to consult the sensor's datasheet to determine the correct pin connections. Many sensors require external power supplies or additional circuitry.

**Connecting Actuators**

Actuators are typically connected to digital output pins. The connections are made using wires or jumper cables. It is important to consult the actuator's datasheet to determine the correct pin connections. Many actuators require external power supplies or additional circuitry.

**Using Libraries :** Libraries are often available to simplify the process of interfacing sensors and actuators with your development board. Libraries provide pre-written code that handles the low-level details of communication with sensors and actuators. Using libraries can save time and effort.

**Best Practices for Interfacing**

- **Consult Datasheets:** Always consult the datasheets of sensors and actuators to determine the correct pin connections and electrical requirements.
- **Use Proper Wiring:** Use proper wiring techniques to ensure reliable connections.
- **Test Connections:** Test the connections before applying power to the circuit.
- **Use External Power Supplies:** Use external power supplies for sensors and actuators that

## READING AND CONTROLLING DATA

**The Heart of Interaction: Data Flow in IoT**

Reading and controlling data is the core functionality of any IoT system. It's the process by which devices sense their environment, process information, and take actions. This involves understanding how to receive data from sensors, interpret it, and then send commands to actuators. The ability to effectively manage this data flow is crucial for creating intelligent and responsive IoT applications. This process involves both hardware and software, and a deep understanding of how both work together.

**Reading Data from Sensors: Analog and Digital Input**

- **Analog Input:**

  - Many sensors, like temperature sensors or light sensors, produce analog signals, which are continuous voltage or current values.

- Development boards like Arduino and Raspberry Pi have analog-to-digital converters (ADCs) that convert these analog signals into digital values that the microcontroller can understand.
- The code for reading analog input involves selecting the appropriate analog input pin, reading the ADC value, and then converting that value into a meaningful unit (e.g., degrees Celsius, lux).
- Calibration is important. Sensors are not always perfectly accurate, and calibration allows for a more precise reading.

- **Digital Input:**

  - Digital sensors, like motion sensors or switches, produce digital signals, which are discrete values (typically 0 or 1).
  - Reading digital input involves selecting the appropriate digital input pin and reading its state.
  - Debouncing is sometimes necessary, especially with mechanical switches, to prevent multiple readings from a single press.
  - Interrupts can be used to trigger code execution when a digital input changes state, allowing for real-time responses.

**Processing and Interpreting Sensor Data**

- **Data Filtering and Smoothing:**

  - Sensor data can be noisy, so it's often necessary to filter and smooth the data to remove unwanted fluctuations.
  - Techniques like moving averages or Kalman filters can be used to smooth data.

- **Data Conversion and Scaling:**

- The raw data from sensors may need to be converted into meaningful units.
- Scaling and calibration are essential for accurate data interpretation.

- **Thresholding and Decision-Making:**

  - Thresholding involves setting limits on sensor values to trigger specific actions.
  - For example, a temperature sensor might trigger an alarm if the temperature exceeds a certain threshold.
  - Logical operators are used to make decisions based on sensor values.

- **Data Logging and Visualization:**

  - Logging sensor data to a file or database allows for analysis and monitoring.
  - Visualization tools can be used to create charts and graphs of sensor data.

### Controlling Actuators: Digital Output and PWM
### Digital Output:

  - Actuators like LEDs or relays are controlled using digital output pins.
  - Setting a digital output pin to HIGH turns the actuator on, and setting it to LOW turns it off.
  - Transistors are often used to amplify the signal from the microcontroller, to control higher powered actuators.

### Pulse Width Modulation (PWM):

  - PWM is used to control the speed of motors or the brightness of LEDs.

- PWM involves rapidly switching a digital output pin on and off, with the duty cycle (the percentage of time the pin is HIGH) determining the average voltage.
- By varying the duty cycle, you can control the speed of a motor or the brightness of an LED.

**Serial Communication:**

- Some actuators are controlled through serial communication protocols like I2C or SPI.
- These protocols allow for more complex control and communication with actuators.

**Real-Time Control and Feedback Loops**

· **Real-Time Control:**

- Many IoT applications require real-time control, where actions are taken immediately in response to sensor data.
- Interrupts and timers can be used to ensure timely execution of code.

· **Feedback Loops:**

- Feedback loops involve continuously monitoring sensor data and adjusting actuator outputs to maintain a desired state.
- PID (proportional-integral-derivative) controllers are commonly used to implement feedback loops.
- Feedback loops allow for complex control of systems, by allowing the system to monitor its own state, and adjust accordingly.

· **Error Handling and Safety:**

- Error handling is crucial for preventing unexpected behavior and ensuring safety.
- Code should include checks for invalid sensor values and actuator states.
- Safety mechanisms, such as limit switches or emergency stops, should be implemented to prevent damage or injury.

Testing is extremely important. Test each sensor input, and actuator output individually, and then test the system as a whole.

# ELEVEN

# BUILDING YOUR FIRST IOT PROJECTS

Having navigated the foundational concepts of IoT and mastered the essentials of setting up your development environment, it's time to bridge the gap between theory and tangible creation. Part III, "Building Your First IoT Projects," is where you'll transform your knowledge into real-world applications, venturing into the exciting realm of practical IoT development. This is where the true magic of IoT unfolds, where abstract concepts become concrete realities, and where you'll experience the satisfaction of seeing your ideas come to life. We're moving beyond the confines of tutorials and examples, stepping into the realm of hands-on experimentation and creative problem-solving. You'll be taking the building blocks of sensors, actuators, and code, and assembling them into functional, interactive systems. This section is designed to be your guide and companion on this exciting journey, empowering you to become a confident and capable IoT maker. We will move from basic projects, to more advanced projects, teaching you along the way.

The most effective way to learn IoT is by doing. We've structured this section around a series of practical projects, each designed to build upon your existing knowledge and introduce new concepts and techniques. You'll start with fundamental projects, like a smart home temperature monitoring system, learning how to interface with sensors, collect data, and visualize it. Then, you'll progress to more interactive projects, such as a remote-controlled LED, exploring the world of actuators and wireless communication. As you gain confidence, you'll tackle more complex applications, like a motion-activated security system, integrating multiple sensors and actuators to create a functional system. We'll guide you through each project with clear, step-by-step instructions, providing code examples, schematics, and troubleshooting tips. We will give you the tools and knowledge to take your projects to the next level, and how to continue to learn on your own. This hands-on approach will not only reinforce your understanding of IoT concepts but also ignite your creativity and inspire you to explore new possibilities.

Building your first IoT projects is just the beginning of your journey. As you progress, you'll discover the vast potential of cloud platforms, enabling you to store, analyze, and visualize data from your devices. We'll introduce you to popular cloud services, demonstrating how to connect your projects to the cloud and leverage its powerful capabilities. We'll also explore the integration of mobile apps, allowing you to control and monitor your IoT devices from anywhere in the world. As you delve deeper into the world of IoT, you'll encounter advanced concepts like edge computing, machine learning, and digital twins, which are shaping the future of connected devices. This section is designed to provide you with a solid foundation, empowering you to explore these advanced concepts and continue your journey of learning and innovation. We will give you the tools to succeed, and to continue to grow as an IoT developer. By the end of this section, you'll have the confidence and skills to tackle your own IoT projects, transforming your ideas into reality and contributing to the ever-expanding world of connected things.

**PROJECT 1: SMART HOME TEMPERATURE MONITORING**

Building a Smart Home Temperature Monitoring system. This isn't just a simple exercise; it's your gateway into the world of practical IoT development. This project will serve as a foundational learning experience, allowing you to solidify your understanding of core IoT concepts and gain practical skills that you'll use in countless future projects. We're starting with a tangible, relatable application – monitoring temperature in a home – because it's a perfect blend of simplicity and real-world relevance. This project is designed to be accessible to beginners, yet it encompasses the essential elements of an IoT system, from sensor integration and data acquisition to data visualization and cloud connectivity. You will be learning the basics of how to build a real world IoT project.

This project will introduce you to the fundamental components that make up an IoT system. You'll learn how to interface with a temperature sensor, a crucial skill for any IoT developer. You'll gain hands-on experience with your chosen microcontroller platform, writing code to read sensor data and process it. You'll understand the flow of data from the physical world, through the sensor, to the microcontroller, and ultimately to a user interface. This process of data acquisition and processing is the heart of IoT, and this project will give you a clear understanding of how it works. We'll cover the basics of wiring, and how to connect the sensor to the microcontroller. We will also cover how to troubleshoot any issues that arise.

Beyond simply collecting data, this project will teach you how to transform raw sensor readings into meaningful insights. You'll learn how to display temperature data in a user-friendly format, whether it's on an LCD screen, a web page, or a mobile app. We'll also introduce you to the power of cloud platforms, demonstrating how to connect your project to the internet and store your data in the cloud. This will allow you to monitor your home's temperature remotely and track historical data. Cloud connectivity is a key aspect of modern IoT applications, and this project will give you a practical introduction to its capabilities. You'll learn how to make the data useful, and how to display it in a meaningful way.

This project is more than just a step-by-step tutorial; it's an opportunity to develop essential problem-solving skills. You'll encounter challenges along the way, and you'll learn how to troubleshoot and debug your code and hardware. This process of overcoming obstacles is a crucial part of the learning experience, and it will prepare you for the complexities of future IoT projects. You'll also learn the importance of planning and organization, as you break down the project into smaller, manageable tasks. The practical skills you gain from this project will form a solid foundation for your IoT development journey, empowering you to tackle more ambitious projects with confidence. We will also cover how to document your project, and how to share it with others.

The Smart Home Temperature Monitoring project is your first step towards building a truly connected living space. By monitoring and controlling your home's environment, you'll experience the convenience and efficiency that IoT can bring. This project is a testament to the power of IoT to transform everyday life, making it more comfortable, efficient, and intelligent. As you progress through this project, remember that you're not just building a temperature monitoring system; you're building a foundation for your future as an IoT developer. This project is designed to be a starting point, to give you the confidence and skills to continue to learn and grow. We encourage you to experiment, explore, and let your creativity guide you as you build your own connected world. This project is the first step in your journey to become an IoT developer.

## HARDWARE SETUP
### (Page 1: Laying the Physical Foundation)

The first step in building your Smart Home Temperature Monitoring system is to set up the hardware. This involves connecting a temperature sensor to your chosen development board, such as an Arduino, Raspberry Pi, or ESP32. A clean and organized hardware setup is crucial for ensuring accurate readings and preventing electrical issues. This phase is about translating your digital design into a physical circuit. We'll be discussing the different types of temperature sensors, and how to select the right one for your project.

**Selecting the Temperature Sensor**

**Types of Sensors:**

- **Thermistors:** These are resistors whose resistance changes with temperature. They are inexpensive and relatively accurate, but require calibration.
- **Thermocouples:** These are made from two different metals that produce a voltage proportional to the temperature difference. They are suitable for high-temperature applications.
- **LM35:** This is an analog temperature sensor that produces a voltage output directly proportional to the temperature. It is easy to use and does not require calibration.
- **DHT11/DHT22:** These sensors measure both temperature and humidity. They are digital sensors that communicate using a serial protocol.
- **DS18B20:** This is a digital temperature sensor that communicates using a 1-Wire protocol. It is accurate and can be used in harsh environments.

**Choosing the Right Sensor:**

- Consider the temperature range, accuracy, and resolution required for your application.
- Choose a sensor that is compatible with your development board.
- Consider the cost and availability of the sensor.

**Connecting the Sensor to the Development Board**

**Analog Sensors:** Connect the sensor's output pin to an analog input pin on the development board. Connect the sensor's power and ground pins to the appropriate pins on the development board. For some sensors, a pull-up or pull-down resistor may be required.

**Digital Sensors:** Connect the sensor's data pin to a digital input/output pin on the development board. Connect the sensor's power and ground pins to the appropriate pins on the development board. For sensors using one wire protocol, a pull up resistor is required.

**Wiring Diagrams:** Use wiring diagrams to ensure that the connections are correct. Double-check the connections before applying power to the circuit.

**Using Breadboards:** Use a breadboard to prototype the circuit before soldering the connections. A breadboard allows for easy connection and disconnection of components.

**Powering the Sensor and Board**

- **Power Supply:**

  - Ensure that the power supply provides the correct voltage and current for the sensor and the development board.
  - Use a stable power supply to prevent fluctuations in sensor readings.

- **Ground Connections:**

  - Connect the ground pins of the sensor and the development board together.
  - A common ground is essential for accurate sensor readings.

- **Voltage Dividers:**

  - If the sensor output voltage is higher than the development board input voltage, use a voltage divider to reduce the voltage.

**Testing the Hardware Setup**

- **Visual Inspection:**

  - Visually inspect the connections to ensure that they are correct.

- **Multimeter Testing:**

- Use a multimeter to check the voltage and current at various points in the circuit.

- **Basic Code Testing:**

  - Write a simple code snippet to read the sensor's raw data and display it on the serial monitor.
  - This will allow you to ensure the sensor is working, and that the board is reading the data.

- **Calibration:**

  - If needed, calibrate the sensor to ensure accurate readings.
  - Calibration involves comparing the sensor readings to a known temperature source.

**Software Development: Writing Code to Read and Display Temperature Data**

The next step is to write the software that will read the data from the temperature sensor and display it. This involves writing code for your chosen development board, using a programming language like C/C++ or Python. The code will read the sensor's output, convert it into a temperature reading, and then display the data on a serial monitor, LCD screen, or other output device. This is where the raw data becomes useful information.

**Reading Sensor Data**

**Analog Sensors:** Use the analogRead() function to read the analog voltage from the sensor's output pin. Convert the analog voltage into a temperature reading using the sensor's datasheet or calibration data.

**Digital Sensors:** Use the digitalRead() function to read the digital signal from the sensor's output pin. Use the appropriate library to communicate with the sensor and retrieve the temperature reading.

**Libraries:** Utilize libraries for the specific sensor being used, as they simplify reading data. Libraries often handle the complex communication protocols for digital sensors.

**Processing and Converting Data**

**Data Conversion:** Convert the raw sensor data into a temperature reading using the appropriate formula or calibration data.

**Data Filtering:** Apply data filtering techniques to remove noise and smooth the temperature readings.

**Data Scaling:** Scale the temperature readings to the desired units (e.g., Celsius, Fahrenheit).

**Displaying the Temperature Data**

- **Serial Monitor:**

  - Use the serial monitor to display the temperature readings.
  - The serial monitor is a useful tool for debugging and testing the code.

- **LCD Screen:**

  - Use an LCD screen to display the temperature readings.
  - LCD screens provide a user-friendly way to display the data.

- **OLED Screen:**

  - Use an OLED screen to display the temperature readings.
  - OLED screens provide a high contrast display.

**Code Optimization and Testing**

- **Code Optimization:**

  - Optimize the code for efficiency and performance.
  - Use appropriate data types and avoid unnecessary calculations.

- **Code Testing:**

  - Test the code thoroughly to ensure that it is working correctly.
  - Use test cases to verify the accuracy of the temperature readings.

- **Error Handling:**

  - Implement error handling to catch and handle any errors that may occur.
  - Handle cases where the sensor returns invalid data.

- **Comments:**

  - Add comments to the code to explain the functionality of each section.
  - Comments make the code easier to understand and maintain.

## CONNECTING TO A CLOUD PLATFORM (E.G., THINGSPEAK) FOR DATA VISUALIZATION

### Extending the Reach of Your Data

Connecting your temperature monitoring system to a cloud platform like ThingSpeak allows you to store, visualize, and analyze your data remotely. This enables you to monitor your home's temperature from anywhere in the world. Cloud platforms also provide features like data logging, alerts, and data analysis tools. This is where your project becomes truly connected.

### Setting Up a ThingSpeak Account

- **Create an Account:**

  - Create a free ThingSpeak account on the MathWorks website.

- **Create a Channel:**

- Create a new channel to store your temperature data.
- Configure the channel fields to match the data you want to store (e.g., temperature).

- **API Keys:**

  - Obtain the API keys for your channel.
  - The API keys are used to authenticate your device and send data to ThingSpeak.

**Modifying the Code to Send Data to ThingSpeak**

- **Include the ThingSpeak Library:**

  - Include the ThingSpeak library in your code.
  - The library provides functions for sending data to ThingSpeak.

- **Enter API Keys:**

  - Enter your ThingSpeak API keys into the code.

- **Send Data:**

  - Use the ThingSpeak library functions to send the temperature data to your channel.
  - Send the data at regular intervals.

**Visualizing the Data on ThingSpeak**

- **Channel Views:**

  - Use the ThingSpeak channel views to visualize your temperature data.
  - ThingSpeak provides various chart types for visualizing data.

- **Widgets:**

  - Use ThingSpeak widgets to create custom dashboards.
  - Widgets allow you to display data in various formats.

- **MATLAB Analysis:**

  - Use MATLAB to analyze your ThingSpeak data.
  - MATLAB provides powerful tools for data analysis and visualization.

### ThingSpeak Features and Considerations

- **Alerts:**

  - Set up alerts to notify you when the temperature exceeds or falls below certain thresholds.
  - Alerts can be sent via email, SMS, or other notification methods.

- **Data Logging:**

  - ThingSpeak automatically logs your data, allowing you to track historical temperature trends.

- **Data Sharing:**

  - Share your ThingSpeak channel with others.
  - This allows others to view your temperature data.

- **API Limits:**

  - Be aware of ThingSpeak's API limits, which restrict the number of data points you can send per minute.

- **Alternatives:**

  - Explore other cloud platforms like AWS IoT Core, Azure IoT Hub, or Google Cloud IoT Core (or related Google Services) if ThingSpeak does not fit your needs.
  - Each platform has its own strengths and weaknesses.

- **Security:**

  - Be mindful of security when sending data to the cloud.
  - Use secure API keys and follow best practices for data security.

## DISPLAYING DATA ON A WEBPAGE

Displaying your temperature data on a webpage makes it easily accessible from any device with an internet connection. This provides a user-friendly way to monitor your home's temperature remotely. This topic will cover the basics of creating a simple webpage to display the data.

**Choosing a Web Technology**

- **HTML, CSS, and JavaScript:**

  - Use HTML to structure the webpage, CSS to style it, and JavaScript to dynamically update the data.
  - This is a common and versatile approach.

- **Web Frameworks:**

  - Consider using a web framework like React, Angular, or Vue.js for more complex web applications.
  - Frameworks can simplify development and provide advanced features.

- **Server-Side vs. Client-Side:**

- ○ Decide whether to use server-side or client-side scripting.
- ○ Server-side scripting involves processing data on a server, while client-side scripting involves processing data in the user's browser

**Retrieving Data from the Sensor or Cloud**

- **Direct Sensor Connection (Local Network):**

  - ○ If your development board is connected to the same local network as your computer, you can retrieve data directly from the board using HTTP requests or other network protocols.
  - ○ This requires setting up a web server on the development board.

- **Cloud Platform (ThingSpeak, etc.):**

  - ○ Use the cloud platform's API to retrieve the temperature data.
  - ○ JavaScript can be used to make API requests and retrieve the data.

- **MQTT:**

  - ○ If you are using a messaging protocol like MQTT to publish the sensor data, you can create a webpage that subscribes to the MQTT topic and displays the data.

**Creating the Webpage**

- **HTML Structure:**

  - ○ Create an HTML file with the basic structure of the webpage.
  - ○ Include elements to display the temperature data.

- **CSS Styling:**

  - Use CSS to style the webpage and make it visually appealing.

- **JavaScript Logic:**

  - Write JavaScript code to retrieve the temperature data and update the webpage.
  - Use AJAX or Fetch API to make asynchronous requests.
  - Use DOM manipulation to update the webpage elements.

- **Real time updates:**

  - Use Javascript setinterval() to create a function that updates the page every set amount of time.

- **Charts and Graphs:**

  - Use JavaScript libraries like Chart.js or D3.js to create charts and graphs of the temperature data.

  **Hosting and Deployment**

- **Local Hosting:**

  - Host the webpage on your local computer using a web server like Apache or Nginx.
  - This is suitable for testing and development.

- **Cloud Hosting:**

  - Host the webpage on a cloud platform like AWS S3, Google Cloud Storage, or Netlify.
  - This makes the webpage accessible from anywhere in the world.

· **Embedded Web Server:**

  - If your development board has sufficient processing power, you can host the webpage directly on the board.
  - This eliminates the need for an external server.

· **Security:**

  - Implement security measures to protect your webpage and data.
  - Use HTTPS to encrypt communication.
  - Sanitize user input to prevent cross-site scripting (XSS) attacks.

· **Mobile Responsiveness:**

  - Ensure that your webpage is mobile-responsive and displays correctly on different screen sizes.

# TWELVE

# WORKING WITH CLOUD PLATFORMS

In the dynamic realm of the Internet of Things (IoT), cloud platforms stand as the expansive horizon, transforming isolated devices into interconnected, intelligent systems. "Working with Cloud Platforms" is not just about connecting to the internet; it's about unlocking the true potential of your IoT projects. The cloud provides a vast, scalable infrastructure that empowers you to transcend the limitations of local processing and storage. It's the place where data transforms from raw sensor readings into actionable insights, where devices become remotely manageable, and where applications gain a level of sophistication previously unattainable. We are moving beyond the confines of basic device functionality and into the realm of distributed intelligence, where data is processed, analyzed, and visualized on a global scale. This section will guide you through the process of harnessing the power of cloud platforms, demonstrating how to seamlessly integrate your IoT projects with these powerful services. We will explore the tools that allow for secure communication, and the methods for data storage and analysis.

The integration of cloud platforms bridges the gap between the physical world of connected devices and the vast potential of data-driven intelligence. It provides the essential infrastructure for data ingestion, storage, processing, and visualization, enabling you to build sophisticated IoT applications that were previously unimaginable. We will explore the functionalities that allow for remote device management, and the techniques for implementing real time data analysis. You will learn how to leverage cloud services for machine learning, enabling your IoT systems to learn and adapt over time. We'll delve into the intricacies of cloud-based security, ensuring that your data and devices are protected from unauthorized access. The cloud acts as a central hub, allowing you to manage and monitor your IoT ecosystem from anywhere in the world. It provides the tools and services you need to build scalable, reliable, and secure IoT solutions. This section is not just about learning to use cloud platforms; it's about understanding how to leverage their capabilities to create truly transformative IoT applications. You will learn how to make your data work for you, and how to use the cloud to create powerful IoT projects

**AWS IOT CORE**

AWS IoT Core is a managed cloud platform that lets connected devices easily and securely interact with cloud applications and other devices. It provides the foundation for building scalable and secure IoT solutions, handling the complexities of device connectivity, data management, and security. It's a comprehensive suite of services that enable you to connect, manage, and scale your IoT devices and applications. AWS IoT Core simplifies the process of building IoT applications by providing a secure and scalable platform for device management, data ingestion, and analysis.

**Key Features and Services**

- **Device Gateway:** Enables secure and efficient communication between devices and the cloud using MQTT, HTTP, and WebSockets.
- **Device Shadow:** Creates a virtual representation of each device in the cloud, allowing applications to interact with devices even when they are offline.

- **Rules Engine:** Allows you to process and route device data to other AWS services, such as Amazon S3, Amazon DynamoDB, and AWS Lambda.
- **IoT Device Management:** Provides tools for onboarding, organizing, monitoring, and remotely managing IoT devices.
- **IoT Analytics:** Enables you to analyze IoT data using SQL queries and build dashboards to visualize insights.
- **IoT Greengrass:** Extends AWS IoT Core functionality to edge devices, enabling local processing and communication.
- **Secure Connectivity:** AWS IoT Core uses mutual authentication and end-to-end encryption to secure communication between devices and the cloud.
- **Integration with other AWS services:** AWS IoT core integrates seamlessly with the vast array of other AWS services.

**Use Cases and Implementation**

- **Industrial IoT (IIoT):** Monitor and control industrial equipment, optimize production processes, and predict maintenance needs.
- **Smart Homes:** Build connected home devices and applications, such as smart thermostats, lighting systems, and security cameras.
- **Connected Vehicles:** Collect and analyze vehicle data, enable remote diagnostics, and provide location-based services.
- **Smart Cities:** Monitor and manage city infrastructure, such as traffic lights, waste management systems, and environmental sensors.
- **Implementation:**

  - Creating device certificates and registering devices with AWS IoT Core.
  - Developing device software to connect to the AWS IoT Core Device Gateway.
  - Configuring AWS IoT Core rules to process and route device data.

- Building applications to interact with devices using the AWS IoT Core APIs.
- Utilizing AWS IoT analytics to create dashboards and reports.

## GOOGLE CLOUD IOT CORE (ALTERNATIVES)

Google Cloud IoT Core has been discontinued, but Google Cloud offers a rich set of services that can be used to build powerful IoT solutions. These services provide the necessary infrastructure for device management, data ingestion, and analysis. This topic will cover the main alternatives to Google Cloud IoT Core. While IoT core is gone, Google's other cloud offerings are still very powerful.

**Key Google Cloud Services for IoT**

- **Pub/Sub:** A real-time messaging service that allows you to ingest and distribute device data.
- **Cloud Functions:** A serverless computing platform that allows you to process and transform device data.
- **BigQuery:** A data warehouse that allows you to store and analyze large volumes of IoT data.
- **Cloud Storage:** A scalable storage service for storing device data and other files.
- **Cloud SQL:** A managed relational database service for storing and querying device data.
- **Vertex AI:** Google Cloud's machine learning platform, which can be used to build and deploy machine learning models for IoT applications.
- **Edge TPU:** Hardware accelerators for running machine learning models on edge devices.
- **Cloud Run:** A serverless platform that allows you to run containerized applications.
- **Chronicle:** A security analytics platform that can be used to monitor and detect security threats in IoT environments.

**Implementing IoT Solutions with Google Cloud**

- **Data Ingestion:** Use Pub/Sub to ingest device data and distribute it to other Google Cloud services.
- **Data Processing:** Use Cloud Functions to process and transform device data in real time.
- **Data Storage and Analysis:** Use BigQuery and Cloud Storage to store and analyze large volumes of IoT data.
- **Machine Learning:** Use Vertex AI to build and deploy machine learning models for IoT applications.
- **Edge Computing:** Use Edge TPU to run machine learning models on edge devices.
- **Security:** Use Chronicle to monitor and detect security threats in IoT environments.
- **Example implementation:**

  - Publishing device data to Pub/Sub topics.
  - Creating Cloud Functions to process and route Pub/Sub messages.
  - Storing and querying device data in BigQuery.
  - Building machine learning models with Vertex AI to predict device failures.

## AZURE IOT HUB

Azure IoT Hub is a managed service hosted in the cloud that acts as a central message hub for bi-directional communication between your IoT application and the devices it manages. It allows you to connect, monitor, and manage millions of IoT assets. Azure IoT Hub simplifies the process of building IoT applications by providing a secure and scalable platform for device management, data ingestion, and analysis.

### Key Features and Services

- **Device Connectivity:** Supports various communication protocols, including MQTT, AMQP, and HTTP.
- **Device Management:** Provides tools for device provisioning, configuration, and monitoring.

- **Device Twins:** Creates a virtual representation of each device in the cloud, allowing applications to interact with devices even when they are offline.
- **IoT Edge:** Extends Azure IoT Hub functionality to edge devices, enabling local processing and communication.
- **Stream Analytics:** Allows you to analyze streaming device data in real time.
- **Azure Functions:** A serverless computing platform that allows you to process and transform device data.
- **Security:** Azure IoT Hub uses mutual authentication and end-to-end encryption to secure communication between devices and the cloud.
- **Integration with other Azure services:** Azure IoT hub is designed to work with the other Microsoft Azure cloud services.

**Use Cases and Implementation**

- **Predictive Maintenance:** Monitor equipment health, predict failures, and optimize maintenance schedules.
- **Remote Monitoring:** Collect and analyze data from remote devices, such as sensors in oil and gas pipelines or wind turbines.
- **Asset Tracking:** Track the location and status of assets, such as vehicles or containers.
- **Smart Agriculture:** Monitor crop health, optimize irrigation, and improve yields.
- **Implementation:**

  - Creating IoT Hub instances and registering devices.
  - Developing device software to connect to Azure IoT Hub.
  - Configuring IoT Hub routes to process and route device data.
  - Building applications to interact with devices using the Azure IoT Hub APIs.
  - Utilizing Azure Stream Analytics to analyze streaming data.

**CREATING AND MANAGING DEVICES IN THE CLOUD**

Creating and managing devices in the cloud is a fundamental aspect of IoT development. Cloud platforms provide tools and services for onboarding, organizing, monitoring, and remotely managing IoT devices. This allows you to scale your IoT deployments and maintain control over your device fleet. This topic will cover the basics of creating and managing devices in the cloud.

**Device Registration and Provisioning**

- **Device Identity:** Each device needs a unique identity to be registered with the cloud platform.
- **Device Certificates:** Device certificates are used to authenticate devices and secure communication.
- **Device Provisioning:** Device provisioning involves registering devices with the cloud platform and configuring their settings.
- **Automatic Provisioning:** Cloud platforms offer automatic provisioning services to simplify the process of registering large numbers of devices.

**Device Management and Monitoring**

- **Device Shadow/Twins:** Cloud platforms use device shadows or twins to create virtual representations of devices in the cloud.
- **Device Configuration:** Cloud platforms allow you to remotely configure device settings.
- **Device Monitoring:** Cloud platforms provide tools for monitoring device health, performance, and status.
- **Remote Updates:** Cloud platforms allow you to remotely update device firmware and software.
- **Device Groups:** Cloud platforms allow you to organize devices into groups for easier management.
- **Security Management:** Cloud platforms provide tools for managing device security, such as certificate rotation and access control.
- **Device Lifecycle Management:** Cloud platforms provide tools for managing the device lifecycle, from registration to

decommissioning.

**Transforming Raw Data into Actionable Insights**

Data storage and analysis are critical components of any IoT solution. Cloud platforms provide scalable and reliable storage services for storing the vast amounts of data generated by IoT devices. They also provide powerful analytics tools for processing and analyzing this data, enabling you to extract valuable insights. This topic will cover the basics of data storage and analysis in the cloud.

# THIRTEEN

# EXPANDING YOUR IOT KNOWLEDGE

The Internet of Things (IoT) is not a static domain; it's a dynamic and rapidly evolving landscape where innovation is the constant. Having journeyed through the fundamentals and built your first projects, you've established a solid foundation. However, the true power of IoT lies in its potential for continuous growth and exploration. "Expanding Your IoT Knowledge" is not merely about accumulating more information; it's about embracing a mindset of lifelong learning, adapting to the ever-shifting tides of technology, and pushing the boundaries of what's possible. The IoT ecosystem is a tapestry woven with threads of diverse technologies, from artificial intelligence and machine learning to edge computing and digital twins. To remain at the forefront of this field, one must be a perpetual student, constantly seeking to deepen their understanding and broaden their skillset. This section is designed to be your compass, guiding you through the advanced concepts and emerging trends that are shaping the future of IoT. We will move beyond the basics, and into the more advanced topics of the field.

As you venture further into the realm of IoT, you'll encounter a plethora of advanced concepts that are revolutionizing the way we interact with connected devices. Edge computing, for instance, is transforming the way data is processed, bringing computation closer to the source and enabling real-time decision-making. Machine learning is empowering IoT systems to learn and adapt, automating tasks and providing predictive insights. Digital twins are creating virtual replicas of physical assets, enabling simulations and optimizations that were previously impossible. Industry 4.0 is leveraging IoT to create smart factories and connected supply chains, driving efficiency and productivity to new heights. We will explore these concepts in depth, providing you with the knowledge and understanding to apply them in your own projects. We will also examine the emerging trends that are shaping the future of IoT, such as the convergence of IoT with blockchain, the rise of low-power wide-area networks (LPWANs), and the increasing focus on security and privacy. These trends are not just theoretical; they are driving real-world applications and creating new opportunities for innovation.

As IoT becomes increasingly pervasive, it's crucial to consider the ethical implications and societal impact of this technology. The vast amounts of data generated by IoT devices raise concerns about privacy, security, and potential misuse. We must grapple with questions of data ownership, algorithmic bias, and the potential for surveillance. Furthermore, the widespread adoption of IoT is transforming industries and reshaping the labor market, raising concerns about job displacement and the need for workforce retraining. We will explore these ethical and societal considerations, fostering a critical and responsible approach to IoT development. We will discuss the importance of building ethical frameworks and regulations that ensure the responsible and equitable use of IoT technologies. We will also examine the role of IoT in addressing global challenges, such as climate change, healthcare, and sustainable development. The impact of IoT is not just technical; it's deeply intertwined with our social fabric.

Expanding your IoT knowledge is not a destination; it's a continuous journey of exploration and discovery. The field of IoT is constantly evolving, with new technologies and applications emerging every day. To remain at the forefront of this field, one must be a lifelong learner, constantly seeking to deepen their understanding and broaden their skillset. We encourage you to embrace a culture of innovation, experimenting with new ideas, and pushing the boundaries of what's possible. We will provide you with resources and guidance to continue your learning journey, including online courses, communities, and open-source projects. We will also highlight the importance of collaboration and knowledge sharing, encouraging you to connect with other IoT enthusiasts and contribute to the growing community. By embracing a mindset of continuous learning and exploration, you can unlock the full potential of IoT and contribute to the creation of a more connected, intelligent, and sustainable world. The journey of IoT development is one of continuous growth and discovery. This section is designed to be a guide, a tool, and a source of inspiration as you continue to expand your knowledge and explore the limitless possibilities of the Internet of Things.

# FOURTEEN

# TROUBLESHOOTING COMMON IOT PROBLEMS

IoT projects, while powerful and transformative, are inherently complex and prone to challenges arising from interconnected devices, diverse communication protocols, and varying environmental conditions. Effective troubleshooting is therefore a crucial skill for any IoT developer. To address these issues, a systematic approach is essential. First, **define the problem** by clearly identifying the symptoms and behavior. Then, **isolate the issue** by breaking down the system into smaller components. **Gather information** such as error messages, sensor readings, and network logs to aid in diagnosis. Next, **formulate hypotheses** based on the gathered information and **test hypotheses** systematically to eliminate potential causes. Once the root cause is identified, **implement a solution** and **verify the solution** thoroughly to ensure the problem is resolved and no new issues have emerged. Finally, **document the solution** for future reference. Common IoT problems include **connectivity issues** with Wi-Fi, Bluetooth, or cellular networks, **sensor malfunctions** causing inaccurate or erratic data, **actuator failures** leading to unresponsive or erratic behavior,

**software errors** such as bugs and syntax issues, **power supply issues** like insufficient voltage, and **environmental factors**such as temperature or humidity. To prevent these problems, implement **thorough testing** of individual components and the system as a whole, perform **regular maintenance**, use **reliable components**, implement **redundancy** in critical areas, **monitor system performance, document system design,** and **keep software updated**. Ultimately, a successful troubleshooter requires **patience and persistence,** strong **analytical thinking,** effective**problem-solving skills**, a commitment to**continuous learning**, and a willingness to **collaborate** with others. Additionally, a well-stocked toolbox of testing equipment is invaluable.

**CONNECTIVITY ISSUES**

Connectivity is the backbone of any IoT system, enabling devices to communicate and exchange data. However, connectivity issues are among the most common problems encountered in IoT deployments. These issues can arise from a variety of sources, including network congestion, signal interference, and configuration errors. This section will cover the most common connectivity issues and provide troubleshooting techniques to resolve them.

**Common Connectivity Issues**

- **Wi-Fi Connectivity:** Problems connecting to Wi-Fi networks, such as incorrect passwords, weak signal strength, or network congestion.
- **Bluetooth Connectivity:** Problems pairing devices, dropped connections, or interference from other Bluetooth devices.
- **Cellular Connectivity:** Problems connecting to cellular networks, such as weak signal strength, roaming issues, or data plan limitations.
- **LoRaWAN Connectivity:** Problems connecting to LoRaWAN gateways, such as signal interference, coverage limitations, or gateway configuration errors.

- **Zigbee Connectivity:** Problems connecting to Zigbee networks, such as signal interference, network congestion, or device pairing issues.
- **MQTT Connectivity:** Problems connecting to MQTT brokers, such as incorrect broker addresses, authentication errors, or network latency.
- **Network Latency:** Delays in data transmission, which can affect real-time applications.
- **Packet Loss:** Loss of data packets during transmission, which can result in incomplete or corrupted data.
- **Firewall Issues:** Firewalls blocking network traffic, which can prevent devices from connecting to the cloud.

**Troubleshooting Techniques for Connectivity Issues**

- **Check Network Configuration:** Verify network settings, such as IP addresses, subnet masks, and gateway addresses.
- **Check Signal Strength:** Use signal strength indicators to assess the strength of Wi-Fi, Bluetooth, or cellular signals.
- **Check Antenna Connections:** Ensure that antenna connections are secure and properly positioned.
- **Check Router and Gateway Settings:** Verify router and gateway settings, such as firewall rules, port forwarding, and network security settings.
- **Check Device Credentials:** Verify device credentials, such as passwords, API keys, and certificates.
- **Use Network Monitoring Tools:** Use network monitoring tools to analyze network traffic and identify connectivity issues.
- **Restart Devices and Network Equipment:** Restart devices and network equipment to refresh network connections.
- **Update Firmware and Software:** Update firmware and software to patch security vulnerabilities and fix bugs.

**Diagnosing Specific Protocol Issues**

- **Wi-Fi:** Check the SSID, password, and security settings. Use a Wi-Fi analyzer to check signal strength and interference.
- **Bluetooth:** Ensure devices are in pairing mode. Check for interference from other Bluetooth devices.
- **Cellular:** Check signal strength and data plan. Contact your cellular provider for assistance.
- **LoRaWAN:** Check gateway coverage and configuration. Use a LoRaWAN network analyzer to check signal strength and packet loss.
- **Zigbee:** Ensure devices are within range and properly paired. Check for interference from other Zigbee devices.
- **MQTT:** Check broker address, port, and credentials. Use an MQTT client to subscribe to topics and monitor messages.

**Advanced Troubleshooting and Tools**

- **Packet Sniffers:** Use packet sniffers like Wireshark to analyze network traffic and identify connectivity issues.
- **Network Analyzers:** Use network analyzers to test network performance and identify bottlenecks.
- **Spectrum Analyzers:** Use spectrum analyzers to identify sources of electromagnetic interference.
- **Ping and Traceroute:** Use ping and traceroute commands to test network connectivity and identify network latency.
- **Log Analysis:** Analyze network logs to identify patterns and anomalies.
- **Remote Access Tools:** Use remote access tools to troubleshoot connectivity issues remotely.

## SENSOR MALFUNCTIONS

Sensors are the eyes and ears of an IoT system, providing crucial data about the environment. However, sensor malfunctions can lead to inaccurate or unreliable data, affecting the performance and reliability of the entire system. This section will cover common sensor malfunctions and provide troubleshooting techniques to resolve them.

## Common Sensor Malfunctions

- **Inaccurate Readings:** Sensor readings that deviate from the expected values.
- **No Readings:** Sensors that fail to provide any data.
- **Erratic Readings:** Sensor readings that fluctuate or change rapidly without any apparent cause.
- **Drift:** Sensor readings that gradually change over time, even when the environment remains constant.
- **Calibration Issues:** Sensors that are not properly calibrated, resulting in inaccurate readings.
- **Environmental Factors:** Sensors that are affected by environmental conditions, such as temperature, humidity, or electromagnetic interference.
- **Wiring Issues:** Sensors that are not properly wired, resulting in incorrect or no readings.
- **Power Supply Issues:** Sensors that are affected by power supply fluctuations or insufficient power.
- **Sensor Damage:** Sensors that are physically damaged, resulting in malfunctions.

## Troubleshooting Techniques for Sensor Malfunctions

- **Check Wiring Connections:** Verify that all wiring connections are secure and properly connected.
- **Check Power Supply:** Ensure that the sensor is receiving the correct voltage and current.
- **Check Sensor Datasheet:** Consult the sensor's datasheet to verify its specifications and operating conditions.
- **Calibrate the Sensor:** Calibrate the sensor to ensure accurate readings.
- **Replace the Sensor:** Replace the sensor if it is damaged or malfunctioning.

- **Use a Multimeter:** Use a multimeter to check the sensor's output voltage or current.
- **Use a Logic Analyzer:** Use a logic analyzer to analyze digital sensor signals.
- **Check for Environmental Factors:** Check for environmental factors that may be affecting the sensor's performance.

## Diagnosing Specific Sensor Issues - continued

- Temperature Sensors: Check for inaccurate readings, drift, or no readings. Verify the sensor's calibration and check for environmental factors such as direct sunlight or airflow.
- Humidity Sensors: Check for inaccurate readings or slow response times. Verify the sensor's calibration and check for condensation or moisture buildup.
- Light Sensors: Check for inaccurate readings or erratic behavior. Check for ambient light interference and verify the sensor's sensitivity.
- Motion Sensors: Check for false triggers or no triggers. Verify the sensor's range and sensitivity settings. Check for obstructions or environmental factors such as air currents or vibrations.
- Pressure Sensors: Check for inaccurate readings or drift. Verify the sensor's calibration and check for leaks or pressure fluctuations.

## Advanced Sensor Troubleshooting and Best Practices

- Data Logging and Analysis: Log sensor data over time to identify patterns and anomalies. Use data analysis tools to visualize and analyze the data.
- Sensor Testing in Controlled Environments: Test sensors in controlled environments to isolate environmental factors.
- Sensor Redundancy: Implement sensor redundancy in critical applications to prevent single points of failure.

- Regular Sensor Calibration: Perform regular sensor calibration to maintain accuracy.
- Sensor Maintenance: Perform regular sensor maintenance, such as cleaning and inspection, to prevent malfunctions.
- Sensor Selection: Choose sensors that are appropriate for the application and environment.
- Noise Reduction: Implement noise reduction techniques, such as filtering and shielding, to improve sensor accuracy.

## SOFTWARE ERRORS

Software errors are a common source of problems in IoT projects. These errors can range from simple syntax errors to complex logic errors that affect the functionality of the entire system. This section will cover common software errors and provide debugging techniques to resolve them.

### Common Software Errors

- Syntax Errors: Errors in the code's syntax, such as missing semicolons or incorrect variable declarations.
- Logic Errors: Errors in the code's logic, such as incorrect conditional statements or loops.
- Runtime Errors: Errors that occur during code execution, such as division by zero or memory access violations.
- Library Errors: Errors related to the use of external libraries, such as incorrect function calls or version incompatibilities.
- Concurrency Errors: Errors that occur when multiple threads or processes access shared resources, such as race conditions or deadlocks.
- Memory Leaks: Errors that occur when memory is allocated but not released, leading to memory exhaustion.
- Buffer Overflows: Errors that occur when data is written beyond the allocated buffer size, potentially leading to security vulnerabilities.
- API Errors: Errors related to the use of APIs, such as incorrect API calls or authentication errors.

## Debugging Techniques

- Serial Monitor/Logging: Use the serial monitor or logging functions to print debugging information, such as variable values and function calls.
- Breakpoints: Use breakpoints to pause code execution and inspect variable values.
- Step-by-Step Execution: Step through the code line by line to identify the source of the error.
- Code Review: Review the code with other developers to identify potential errors.
- Unit Testing: Write unit tests to verify the functionality of individual code modules.
- Integration Testing: Write integration tests to verify the interaction between different code modules.
- Debugging Tools: Use debugging tools, such as debuggers and profilers, to identify and resolve software errors.
- Error Messages: Carefully read and analyze error messages to identify the source of the problem.

## Diagnosing Specific Software Issues

- Syntax Errors: Check for syntax errors in the code editor or compiler output.
- Logic Errors: Use the serial monitor or debugging tools to trace the code's execution and identify logical errors.
- Runtime Errors: Analyze error messages and use debugging tools to identify the source of the runtime error.
- Library Errors: Check the library documentation and ensure that the library is compatible with the development environment.
- Concurrency Errors: Use thread synchronization techniques to prevent race conditions and deadlocks.
- Memory Leaks: Use memory profiling tools to identify memory leaks.

- Buffer Overflows: Use buffer overflow detection tools to identify potential vulnerabilities.
- API Errors: Check the API documentation and verify the API calls and authentication credentials.

**Best Practices for Software Development**

- Write Clean and Readable Code: Write code that is easy to understand and maintain.
- Use Meaningful Variable Names: Use variable names that clearly indicate their purpose.
- Add Comments to the Code: Add comments to the code to explain the functionality of each section.
- Use Version Control: Use version control systems, such as Git, to track code changes and collaborate with other developers.
- Follow Coding Standards: Follow established coding standards to ensure consistency and readability.
- Test the Code Thoroughly: Test the code thoroughly to identify and resolve errors before deployment.
- Implement Error Handling: Implement error handling to catch and handle errors gracefully.
- Use Libraries and Frameworks: Use well-tested libraries and frameworks to simplify development.

**Debugging Techniques**

Debugging is an essential skill for any IoT developer. It involves the systematic process of identifying and resolving software and hardware errors. This section will cover various debugging techniques that can be used to troubleshoot IoT problems.

**Debugging Tools and Techniques**

- Serial Monitor/Logging: Print debugging information to the serial monitor or log files.
- Breakpoints: Pause code execution at specific points to inspect variable values.

- Step-by-Step Execution: Step through the code line by line to identify the source of the error.
- Watch Variables: Monitor the values of variables during code execution.
- Logic Analyzers: Analyze digital signals to identify timing and logic errors.
- Multimeters: Measure voltage, current, and resistance to identify hardware issues.
- Oscilloscopes: Visualize electrical signals to identify signal integrity issues.
- Packet Sniffers: Analyze network traffic to identify communication errors.
- Debuggers: Use debugging tools to step through code, set breakpoints, and inspect variables.
- Profilers: Use profiling tools to identify performance bottlenecks.

**Debugging Process**

- Identify the Problem: Clearly define the symptoms and behavior of the problem.
- Isolate the Issue: Break down the system into smaller components to isolate the source of the problem.
- Gather Information: Collect relevant information, such as error messages, sensor readings, and network logs.
- Formulate Hypotheses: Develop possible explanations for the problem based on the gathered information.
- Test Hypotheses: Systematically test each hypothesis to eliminate potential causes.
- Implement a Solution: Once the root cause is identified, implement a solution to fix the problem.
- Verify the Solution: Test the system thoroughly to ensure that the problem is resolved and that no new problems have been introduced.

- Document the Solution: Document the problem, the solution, and the steps taken to resolve it.

## Debugging Strategies

- Top-Down Debugging: Start by debugging the top-level components and then move down to the lower-level components.
- Bottom-Up Debugging: Start by debugging the lower-level components and then move up to the top-level components.
- Divide and Conquer: Break down the problem into smaller, more manageable parts.
- Binary Search: Use a binary search approach to narrow down the source of the error.
- Rubber Duck Debugging: Explain the code to an inanimate object, such as a rubber duck, to identify logical errors.

## Advanced Debugging Techniques and Best Practices

- Remote Debugging: Debug code running on remote devices.
- Post-Mortem Debugging: Analyze crash dumps and log files to identify the cause of a crash.
- Static Analysis: Use static analysis tools to identify potential errors in the code without running it.
- Dynamic Analysis: Use dynamic analysis tools to monitor the code's behavior during execution.
- Test-Driven Development (TDD): Write tests before writing code to ensure that the code meets the requirements.
- Continuous Integration/Continuous Delivery (CI/CD): Use CI/CD pipelines to automate the testing and deployment process.
- Debugging Mindset: Develop a systematic and analytical approach to debugging.
- Patience and Persistence: Debugging can be a time-consuming process, requiring patience and persistence.

# FIFTEEN

# RESOURCES FOR FURTHER LEARNING

The journey into the Internet of Things (IoT) is not a destination, but a continuous expedition. While this guide has provided a solid foundation, the true depth and breadth of IoT knowledge extend far beyond its pages. "Resources for Further Learning" is your navigational chart for this expansive universe, a guide to the tools and platforms that will fuel your ongoing exploration. The field of IoT is dynamic, constantly evolving with new technologies, protocols, and applications. To remain relevant and innovative, you must embrace a mindset of perpetual learning, actively seeking out new information and honing your skills. This section is designed to serve as your compass, pointing you towards the diverse resources that will empower you to deepen your understanding and expand your expertise. We will explore the many ways to keep learning, and the places that can help you do so.

Building a robust IoT knowledge base requires more than just passive consumption of information. It necessitates active engagement with a diverse ecosystem of learning resources. Online courses, tutorials, communities, forums, open-source projects, books, and articles – each plays a vital role in shaping your understanding and fostering your growth. This section will guide you through the process of curating your own personalized learning ecosystem. We will delve into how to critically evaluate online courses, identify active and supportive IoT communities, leverage the power of open-source projects, and select relevant books and articles. We'll emphasize the importance of hands-on experimentation, encouraging you to apply your knowledge by building your own projects and contributing to open-source initiatives. Furthermore, we will show you how to identify the resources that fit your specific learning style, and how to create a learning plan that works best for you. This active approach will transform you from a passive learner into a proactive explorer, capable of navigating the ever-changing landscape of IoT.

The IoT community is a vibrant and collaborative space where individuals from diverse backgrounds come together to share knowledge, solve problems, and drive innovation. "Resources for Further Learning" highlights the importance of connecting with this community, whether through online forums, social media groups, or local meetups. Collaboration is essential for navigating the complexities of IoT, as it allows you to learn from the experiences of others and contribute your own unique insights. By participating in open-source projects, you can collaborate with developers from around the world, contributing to the development of cutting-edge IoT solutions. Moreover, we will explore the importance of mentorship and knowledge sharing. Connecting with experienced IoT professionals can provide valuable guidance and support, helping you to overcome challenges and accelerate your learning journey. This section emphasizes that learning is not a solitary pursuit, but a collaborative endeavor. By embracing the power of community and collaboration, you can unlock the full potential of IoT and contribute to the creation of a more connected, intelligent, and sustainable world. Your active participation in the community can help to shape the future of IoT.

## ONLINE COURSES AND TUTORIALS

**The Digital Classroom: Democratizing IoT Education**

Online courses and tutorials have revolutionized how we learn about IoT, making it accessible to anyone with an internet connection. These resources provide structured learning paths, interactive exercises, and expert instruction, allowing you to learn at your own pace and from the comfort of your own home. They democratize education, removing geographical and financial barriers to entry, making IoT knowledge widely available.

**Types of Online Courses and Platforms**

- Massive Open Online Courses (MOOCs): Platforms like Coursera, edX, and Udacity offer MOOCs from top universities and industry experts. These courses often cover a wide range of IoT topics, from fundamental concepts to advanced applications.
- Specialized IoT Platforms: Platforms like Arduino Create, Raspberry Pi Foundation, and Adafruit offer tutorials and courses tailored to their specific hardware and software.
- Video Tutorials: YouTube and other video platforms host a vast library of free tutorials on various IoT topics. Channels like GreatScott!, DroneBot Workshop, and Andreas Spiess provide valuable hands-on demonstrations and explanations.
- Interactive Coding Platforms: Websites like Codecademy and freeCodeCamp offer interactive coding tutorials that allow you to practice your programming skills in real-time.
- Vendor-Specific Training: Companies like Amazon (AWS), Google (Google Cloud), and Microsoft (Azure) offer training and certifications on their IoT cloud platforms.

**Evaluating and Choosing Online Courses**

- Instructor Credentials: Research the instructor's background and expertise in IoT.
- Course Curriculum: Review the course syllabus to ensure that it covers the topics you are interested in.

- Course Reviews: Read reviews from other students to get an idea of the course's quality and effectiveness.
- Hands-on Projects: Look for courses that include hands-on projects and practical exercises.
- Community Support: Check if the course offers community support, such as forums or discussion groups.
- Cost and Time Commitment: Consider the cost of the course and the time commitment required.
- Certification: Determine if the course offers a certificate of completion.

**Recommended Online Courses and Tutorials**

- Introduction to the Internet of Things (Coursera): A comprehensive course covering the fundamentals of IoT.
- Building IoT Solutions with Raspberry Pi (edX): A hands-on course focused on building IoT projects with Raspberry Pi.
- AWS IoT Core Essentials (AWS Training): A course on using AWS IoT Core for building IoT applications.
- Azure IoT Developer (Microsoft Learn): A learning path covering Azure IoT Hub and other Azure IoT services.
- Arduino Getting Started Tutorials (Arduino Create): A collection of tutorials for beginners using Arduino.
- Raspberry Pi Getting Started Tutorials (Raspberry Pi Foundation): A collection of tutorials for beginners using Raspberry Pi.
- YouTube Channels: GreatScott!, DroneBot Workshop, Andreas Spiess, and many more.

**Maximizing Your Learning Experience**

- Set Clear Goals: Define your learning objectives and track your progress.
- Take Notes: Take detailed notes and summarize key concepts.

- Practice Regularly: Practice coding and building projects regularly to reinforce your learning.
- Participate in Discussions: Engage in discussions with other students and instructors.
- Build Your Own Projects: Apply your knowledge by building your own IoT projects.
- Stay Up to Date: Keep up with the latest IoT trends and technologies.
- Join Study Groups: Form study groups to learn and collaborate with other learners.

## IOT COMMUNITIES AND FORUMS

IoT communities and forums provide a valuable platform for connecting with other IoT enthusiasts, sharing knowledge, and getting help with your projects. These online spaces foster collaboration, problem-solving, and continuous learning, making them an essential resource for any IoT developer. They provide a space to ask questions, and learn from other's experiences.

### Types of IoT Communities and Forums

- Online Forums: Forums like the Arduino Forum, Raspberry Pi Forums, and Stack Overflow provide a space for asking questions and getting help with specific problems.
- Social Media Groups: Facebook groups, LinkedIn groups, and Reddit communities provide a platform for sharing information and connecting with other IoT enthusiasts.
- Open-Source Project Communities: Communities associated with open-source IoT projects, such as Home Assistant and ESPHome, provide support and resources for users.
- Maker Spaces and Hackerspaces: Physical spaces where makers and hackers gather to work on projects and share knowledge.
- Meetup Groups: Local Meetup groups focused on IoT provide opportunities for networking and learning.
- Vendor-Specific Communities: Companies like Amazon, Google, and Microsoft have online communities for their IoT cloud

platforms.

## Benefits of Joining IoT Communities

- Get Help with Problems: Ask questions and get help from experienced IoT developers.
- Share Knowledge: Share your knowledge and experience with others.
- Learn from Others: Learn from the experiences and insights of other community members.
- Network with Professionals: Connect with other IoT professionals and build your network.
- Stay Up to Date: Stay up to date with the latest IoT trends and technologies.
- Find Inspiration: Get inspired by the projects and ideas of other community members.
- Collaborate on Projects: Collaborate with other community members on open-source projects.

## Recommended IoT Communities and Forums

- Arduino Forum: A forum for Arduino users of all skill levels.
- Raspberry Pi Forums: A forum for Raspberry Pi users of all skill levels.
- Stack Overflow (IoT Tag): A question and answer site for IoT-related questions.
- Reddit (r/iot, r/arduino, r/raspberry_pi): Reddit communities for IoT-related discussions.
- Home Assistant Community: A community for users of the Home Assistant open-source home automation platform.
- ESPHome Community: A community for users of the ESPHome open-source firmware for ESP devices.
- Maker Spaces and Hackerspaces: Search for local maker spaces and hackerspaces in your area.

### Participating in IoT Communities

- Be Respectful: Be respectful and courteous to other community members.
- Ask Clear Questions: Ask clear and specific questions to get the best answers.
- Share Your Knowledge: Share your knowledge and experience with others.
- Contribute to Discussions: Participate in discussions and offer your insights.
- Follow Community Guidelines: Follow the community guidelines and rules.
- Give Back to the Community: Contribute to open-source projects and help other community members.
- Attend Meetups and Events: Attend local meetups and events to network with other IoT enthusiasts.

### OPEN-SOURCE IOT PROJECTS

Open-source IoT projects provide a valuable resource for learning and building IoT applications. These projects offer access to source code, documentation, and community support, allowing you to learn from the work of others and contribute to the development of innovative IoT solutions. They provide a hands on way to learn by doing.

### Types of Open-Source IoT Projects

- Home Automation Platforms: Platforms like Home Assistant and OpenHAB provide open-source solutions for home automation.
- Embedded Firmware: Projects like ESPHome and Tasmota provide open-source firmware for ESP devices.
- IoT Cloud Platforms: Projects like ThingsBoard and Eclipse IoT provide open-source IoT cloud platforms.
- Sensor Libraries: Libraries like the Adafruit Sensor Library and the Arduino Sensor Library provide open-source code for interfacing with various sensors.

- Communication Protocols: Projects like MQTT and CoAP provide open-source implementations of IoT communication protocols.
- Data Visualization Tools: Tools like Grafana and InfluxDB provide open-source solutions for visualizing IoT data.
- Operating Systems: Operating systems like Linux and FreeRTOS are often used in IoT projects.

## Benefits of Using Open-Source IoT Projects

- Access to Source Code: Access to source code allows you to learn how IoT applications are built.
- Community Support: Open-source projects often have active communities that provide support and resources.
- Cost-Effective: Open-source projects are often free to use, reducing the cost of development.
- Customization: Open-source projects can be customized to meet your specific needs.
- Collaboration: Open-source projects encourage collaboration and knowledge sharing.
- Transparency: Open-source projects are transparent, allowing you to inspect the code and identify potential issues.
- Innovation: Open-source projects often drive innovation and development in the IoT field

## Recommended Open-Source IoT Projects

- **Home Assistant:** An open-source home automation platform.
- **ESPHome:** An open-source firmware for ESP devices.

# SIXTEEN
## CONCLUSION

As we reach the culmination of this comprehensive guide, "IoT for Beginners: A Step-by-Step Guide," we reflect on the journey undertaken, from the initial understanding of IoT's core principles to the practical application of building your first connected projects. This guide has aimed to demystify the complexities of the Internet of Things, providing a structured pathway for beginners to navigate the vast landscape of interconnected devices and data. You've learned to set up your development environment, interface with sensors and actuators, harness the power of cloud platforms, and troubleshoot common challenges. This foundational knowledge is not merely a collection of technical skills; it's a gateway to a world of innovation, creativity, and problem-solving. We have given you the tools to create, and the knowledge to grow.

The goal of this guide has been to empower you, the beginner, to become an active participant in the IoT revolution. By breaking down complex concepts into digestible steps and providing practical examples, we've aimed to foster a sense of confidence and competence. You've gained the ability to translate your ideas into tangible IoT projects, from simple temperature monitoring systems to more sophisticated applications that leverage cloud connectivity and data analysis. This newfound ability is not just about building gadgets; it's about understanding how technology can be used to solve real-world problems and improve our lives. The skills you've acquired are the building blocks for future innovations, enabling you to contribute to the ever-expanding world of connected things. We hope that this guide has lit a spark, and created a desire to keep learning.

The field of IoT is in a constant state of flux, with new technologies and applications emerging at an accelerating pace. This guide has provided you with a solid foundation, but the journey of learning and discovery is far from over. The importance of lifelong learning cannot be overstated. As you continue to explore the world of IoT, you'll encounter advanced concepts like edge computing, machine learning, and digital twins, which are shaping the future of connected devices. Embrace the challenge of continuous learning, stay curious, and seek out opportunities to expand your knowledge. Attend workshops, participate in online communities, and experiment with new technologies. The IoT ecosystem thrives on collaboration and knowledge sharing, so don't hesitate to connect with other enthusiasts and contribute to the growing community. Your learning is just beginning.

As IoT becomes increasingly integrated into our lives, it's crucial to consider the ethical implications and societal impact of this technology. The vast amounts of data generated by connected devices raise concerns about privacy, security, and potential misuse. We must strive to build IoT systems that are not only innovative but also responsible and ethical. This involves designing systems that are secure, transparent, and respectful of user privacy. It also involves considering the environmental impact of IoT devices and promoting sustainable practices. As you continue your IoT journey, remember to prioritize ethical considerations and strive to create solutions that benefit society as a whole. Your work has the potential to help create a better future.

You are now equipped with the knowledge and skills to contribute to the dawn of a connected future. The IoT landscape is vast and full of opportunities for innovation. Your creativity, problem-solving skills, and passion for technology can help shape the future of IoT, creating solutions that address real-world challenges and improve the quality of life for people around the globe. Don't be afraid to experiment, explore new ideas, and push the boundaries of what's possible. Embrace the challenges, learn from your mistakes, and celebrate your successes. The world of IoT is waiting for your contributions. We encourage you to continue to learn, and to share your knowledge with the world. The future of IoT is in your hands.